T0146441

Pure, Poetic Poetry

<u>Pure</u>, <u>Poetic</u> <u>Poetry</u>

By: _theshy1

PURE, POETIC POETRY

iUniverse books may be ordered through booksellers or by contacting:

iUniverse
1663 Liberty Drive
Bloomington, IN 47403
www.iuniverse.com
1-800-Authors (1-800-288-4677)

ISBN: 978-1-5320-3456-5 (sc)
ISBN: 978-1-5320-3457-2 (e)

Print information available on the last page.

iUniverse rev. date: 09/27/2019

*I'm Pure, I'm Poetic
and This Is My Poetry*

I'm Pure, I'm Poetic
and This Is My Poetry

I'm Pure, I'm Poetic
and This Is My Poetry

Dedicated To:
Tupac Shakur
Your Words Inspired Me.

Also, To My Mother, Carlotta
Who Never Stopped Believing In Me,
I Thank You and Love You.

I'm Pure, I'm Poetic
and This Is My Poetry

**I'm Pure, I'm Poetic
and This Is My Poetry**

Pure, Poetic Poetry

Table Of Contents:

~Idol Section:~

~Mama's Section:~

~Daddy's Section:~

~Sister's Section:~

~Brother's Section:~

~Family & Friends Section:~

~Inspirational Section:~

~My Section:~

~My Thank You's:~

You better read that, you might be in there

Extra's

Idol Section

<u>Why I Write</u>

Nothing Was Wasted:

I wrote **Nothing Was Wasted** because I wanted to write something in memory of Aaliyah to show that I admired her talent and the person she was. I wanted to show that she touched me, not just with her voice and her acting but with her heart and soul. She taught me that family was more important than money, she showed me that it's alright to stay humble and grounded, to keep joking and always be myself. I thank her for that. Now I drew a picture of her as well, a photo that she did in "Honey Magazine" for the November 2001 issue but I knew there was a good chance that no one would ever see that so I did the poem hoping that one day somebody would read it. I wish I had the opportunity to meet her, but since I didn't, I hope that this will touch her wherever she is. She was my favorite before she died and she always will be.

Nothing Was Wasted

Written For
The Memory Of Aaliyah

A...

Line 1   A life destined to shine beyond the sunlight

Line 2   A life worshiped by a true belief of what's promised for you

A...

Line 1   An eye blinded by the shine in the night

Line 2   An eye hid behind shades just to focus on what you went through

L...

Line 1   Like many stars, life had its chance to shoot across the sky

Line 2   Like many I watched and cheered life beyond streams

I...

Line 1   I among them looked up to the possibilities in hopes to try

Line 2   I among so many to accomplish our hopeless dreams

Y...

Line 1   Your goal was seen to be truthful and never ending

Line 2   Your aim to be more than just
"camera - faced"

A...

Line 1   After all, you demand to be loved for
being real and depending

Line 2   After all, to show your truth with no
time to waste

H...

Line 1   HE had to take you to show what you
improved

Line 2   HE had to make you see what you changed

F...

Line 1   For if we thought about death and not
life no one would move

Line 2   For if you hadn't existed, my dreams
would be all out of range

A...

Line 1   And because of the life you led and
what you left behind

Line 2   And because your life although short
it was fulfilling

N...

Line 1   New life begins in the position of what
was set in your mind

Line 2   New life of that "Gum Angel" that was
capable and willing

S...

Line 3   Shows nothing was wasted.

<u>Why I Write</u>

Your Music Helped Me Too:

I wrote **Your Music Helped Me Too**, in memory of my favorite rapper of all time, Tupac Shakur. Half of the inspiration for me wanting to write, I read "The Rose That Grew From Concrete," and I was hooked from then on. I loved the way he expressed his life through music as well as his poetry, which is the same thing without a beat. I believe that God put him here to touch our hearts no matter his methods and He definitely succeeded in having him reach mine because I feel that I can do anything with the talents that God gave me and I am going to try to exceed at every last one of them. So if one fails, then on to the next one. Tupac taught me that, with his soul and hopefully one day I will show that to someone, with mine.

Your Music Helped Me Too

Written For
The Memory Of Tupac Shakur

No words that I know can describe how you've inspired us
No one alive can fill your space
If you could get our radio stations where you are I'm pretty sure; you will hear all the male rappers are all making a fuss
About who sounds more like you or rhymes like you and this guy 50 Cent comes pretty close and has a lot of similar life experiences too but he will never take your place
You came into my life a little earlier than "Keep Your Head Up," but that's when you made the biggest impact
I was so use to women standing up for women, but it felt good when I heard a man standing up for women thanks
From that day on you were always on my tapes, you were always in my CD player, and I only listened to the radio if you were on it
Listening to you made me realize that I could always step forward and didn't have to look back
You taught me that people can learn from the things that they've been through and that I should stay by my mama no matter what she's going or has gone through because she will always be by my side when my bad times call
You were my inspiration for writing poetry, I mean after reading The Rose That Grew From Concrete

I started thinking that if I don't get to voice my opinions as you did, being famous and all, I wanted to leave something behind to show that I feel things and I'm not always about joking around

When this is found and read out loud, I want people to feel my words, relate to them and learn from them and that's what I think you were trying to do with your music

While "some people" wouldn't give your words a chance, not knowing that making a big deal out of them, would only make us want to listen to you more

I'm glad that you were around in my generation because without your music we, "the fans," would probably never know what Hip Hop (rap) to the next level was and would probably never hear that pure sound

I thank you for being an influence in our lives especially mine and even though I didn't get my chance to meet you while you were here I honestly think that wherever you are, you can spread your wings and soar, Love you.

<u>Why I Write</u>

Jigga Is Still That Nigga:

I wrote **<u>Jigga Is Still That Nigga</u>** because he is. He filled that empty void left by Tupac (now he holds the "Best Rapper Passed" title). I never thought anyone would catch my ear or my attention like Tupac did, even though they are different in style and approach but I like him. It was crazy when Jay Z said he was retiring, but you should have seen how excited I was when he came back, I went out and bought the CD immediately. But most of my CD's got stolen so I can't claim that anymore. So now I legally download everything from Reasonably Doubt to wherever it will end. I have yet to go to one of his concerts, though I was surprised and happy when my cousins and I went to the "Ladies First Tour" and he came out at the end with Beyoncé, good times. Hope I get to meet you at least once, cause I didn't get the chance to meet Aaliyah or Tupac so if I get the chance, I'm taking it.

Jigga Is Still That Nigga

Written For
Jay Z

I had damn near all your albums
And I could listen to them all day at any volume
Still, I want more
However, there is no more
Or
I mean there are the ones that didn't make the cut
And if you did them, then they gotta be as good
as "Nigga What?"
But
That's up to you to bring them out
I'm sure you've had a request like this for you to
keep making music, so you know what I'm talking
about
But this is more like you bringing out the old
instead of the new
I mean I would prefer to hear something new but
as long as it's still you
Everything is all good
Cause anything from you will still be all hood
And that's why we love you so much
Listening to you is like walking on a broken leg
and needing no crutch
That feeling free to do anything is what I like
Thank you for being here rapping through my
generation cause it felt right
See when Tupac was here, he was my favorite living
rapper

And when he died, I saw rap heading straight towards the crapper
But then I heard you doing your thing
And I felt allergic and swollen from your sting
But I still couldn't get enough
Cause whatever you stung me with, it filled me up
And it made me crave your best
And I know you're tired, but I don't think you can give up all this and just rest
Cause like Tupac; no one will ever fill your shoes
The best stays the best like the Carnival Cruise
I mean I don't know, these are just my thoughts
A release of my feelings to smooth out the knots
So do with this what you will
Just know that you will always be "The Man" to me and that's real.

I am glad that you realized that music is one of the best ways to express yourself
Even without reading my suggestion, you had your own food for thought to keep you in good health.

Why I Write

Only Him:

I wrote **<u>Only Him</u>** because, well that's easy... How can I write all of these poems and not give thanks or show appreciation to the highest being, the one who gave me the talent and blessings to do this? I can't do anything without Him; no one can, so when it comes right down to it He is my hands, He is my mind, my thoughts, He's my heart and my feelings. He is me, and I am Him, nothing more or nothing less and nothing in between.

Only Him

Written To
Show Appreciation To
The Creator

He gave me life
He picked my soul
He helped me live
He made me whole
He watches over me
He keeps me safe
He listens to me
He's why I keep the faith
He gives me love
He sees me fall
He lifts me up
He dusts me off
He showed me the way
He waited for me to choose my path
He guided me towards the good
He shielded me from the bad
He lights my world when it goes dim
He is my one and only
He knows there is no one like Him
He takes me to my limit
He knows my destiny
He is the Creator, my Father
And He always will be.

Mama's Section

<u>Why I Write</u>

Disappearing Footsteps:

I wrote **<u>Disappearing Footsteps</u>** because I wanted to.., not hurt but bring awareness to what a habit as vicious as that one was doing to not only me but the family. I wanted to show how it could be if we followed in the footsteps that were left behind. I was just in my feelings at the time, and I think it was good to get them out cause I think it was beneficial and probably got the ball rolling to the end of something sad before it turned into something horrible.

Disappearing Footsteps

Written For
My Mama

It came after you, now it's coming after us
We followed your footsteps and found out what
it was
Things happen that are sometimes hard to take
care of
But some things are more important than getting
a buzz
No, my thang ain't rapping and my name ain't 50
(Cent)
But what would I know about life getting shifty
Only that Sister is sprung out on it and Brother's
getting there
How would you feel if I started selling my body
for drug-fare
Life is too short to be effing it up
With something that can only make you more corrupt
What if I followed your footsteps of that drug
life too
And made you realize what it can really do
How it can make your family not want to help
Show you, from time to time how I felt
I'm not writing this to show you that we don't
care
But I wanted to know if you would change on a
double dare
Because I can't stand to see you hurt yourself,
it's not fair
Living everyday like it should be your last

If I'm wrong then we will let the past be the past
I just think you're smarter than the president
To be throwing your life away like pieces of lent
This poem was written to show you how you're
hurting my life
I want you to live long enough to see me become
a wife
Have kids and make the money that I've always
dreamed of
Buy you things that show you the real love
Love that comes from family not from friends
The type that's real, not the kind that depends
Depends on your money or your stash
Something along the lines of Aaliyah and Mr. Dash
True and peaceful and not in your depths
So all I'm asking of you is to erase your footsteps
So that even you can't follow them.

Why I Write

Remember:

I wrote **<u>Remember</u>** because I wanted to reminisce on the good old days, the not so good days and I felt that it wouldn't be right to look back at the good and not remember at least 1 or 2 days of the bad. Plus, it kind of shows a timeline of how I thought that I was maybe part of the reason for my mama's downward spiral, I mean just because I wasn't the one to start it off I still felt that I wasn't making it better by leaving. I cried when I wrote this poem, and every time I go back and read it, I cry. Those were some hard times for me to remember.

Remember

Written For
My Mama

Remember?
Remember when I was little and you worked
at the post office and we all lived with daddy?
Now I know that's not a memory that you
want to remember but work with me for a
minute because there's something important that
went on then. That's when I would sit right
in front of the door as soon as I woke up
and stayed there until you came home.
I miss those days.

Remember?
Remember when we moved away from daddy
and it was all of us together, you, me, Landon
and Carla? Then Carla left and Landon not that
far after,
probably thinking that their lives would be
better
with a man that might never lose his job and
would give them whatever they needed when they
needed it and all they would have to do is suffer
through him cursing them out whenever he wanted
to, maybe even thinking that they would make
it now.
Or remember me sticking by you when all
of your hard times came all at once. I never left
your side because I knew that there was no

other place I would rather be. I wanted to be
there to
help you see, that just because you felt that
there was nothing
you could do right, I wanted to be there to
remind you that your life wasn't a waste to
everybody.
I miss those days too.

Remember?
Remember when I wanted to go to West Meck
with my cousin's but for me to do
that I would have to leave you and move back
in with daddy? Did you know that was the
hardest thing that I had to do? Going when no one
else was there for you, and I wish that I
could live that day over again so I could change
my decision because from that day on I think that
your life started to take a turn for the worst. No
matter how you tried to hide it from me I could
feel that something wasn't right and I didn't
need to listen to someone else because I could
see it for me, all by myself.
I wish those days didn't exist.

Remember?
Remember how you felt when you told me not
to visit you or when you said to me that you
wasn't coming to visit me? Did it hurt or make
you feel confused any of those times? Did it make
you mad going more days without seeing us because
that's how I felt when I knew there would be more
days in between our next visit and because
we will never know when God is going to come and
take one of us with Him to Heaven,
I would like to see you before that day.

Cause I miss you. I honestly can't remember how it felt to see you pleased with life and feel that you were happy.
Can you...
remember?

Why I Write

Seeing Clear:

I wrote **<u>Seeing Clear</u>** because I'm not going to lie, I was mad that things and people came before my siblings and me. I know "mama gotta have a life too" but it's some things that are more important than the life you were leading. A guy that is not important enough to be considered your "man" clearly shows that he ain't important enough to push us to the side for, and I know that I can never understand the feeling you got from your habit, but that wasn't important either. I wish she could have seen or heard how we felt, so I wrote what I felt.

<u>Seeing Clear</u>

Written For
The Choices You Make

Why when we make plans to do something more than
just eat food
You are always waiting on one of your dudes
And then when you agree to do things with us
It's just so easy for them to take you away from us
I mean do you really think your car, your friends
or even your sex life is more important than your
kids
Shit, no that can't be what you think
Cause you beg for our attention
Also, I would love to see you every day; my
siblings take it as if they just got detention
Damn haters
And what's up with all these men you know but none
of them are considered being a dater
All I'm saying is it's hard to count how many
times you've broken the plans
Seriously, do you think that you can make the
situation better by the clap of your hands
Hell no, I said hell no
Cause there is a piece of my heart that breaks
off every time you just go
Damn near 11 years all that time I've lived with
you making these decisions
And trust me, growing up looking towards the
future this was not in my visions
So I guess no matter what that's just how you're
gonna be

And there's nothing in this world, not even these
words that can make you change your destiny
Because it's your life, your choices
And all we can do is speak, it's up to you to
hear our voices
So I'm saying if you don't want this to be
something that I fear
All you have to do is open your eyes and start
seeing clear.

Why I Write

Finally:

I wrote **Finally** because out of all the poems I wrote for and about my mama, this is the one that shows how proud I was for her to get over her struggles with drugs finally. I don't know if I was apart of her decision to do it but I like to think so, but if not, I can give credit where credit is due. I'm glad that she finally decided that it was time to stop and what I said was right, if you find yourself in the corner of people that said they would help but aren't, then you can always turn to me, and I'll do any and everything in my powers to help you.

Finally

_Written For
The Best Day Ever_

Found footsteps
Just yours and His
No crumbs left over to lead any followers
Hoped and prayed but I never thought I'd see the
day where my mama would finally be clean

Recovered memories
Good thoughts, thought of
Great times remembered
Hoped and prayed but I never thought my mama
would finally see, to others, what her life truly
means

Focused eyes
No more blurry visions
Better future in sight
Hoped and prayed but I never thought my mama
would finally realize her life was worth being
seen

And finally
Hope has become reality
Answered Prayers
Always thought my mama would finally see she was
and still will be a queen.

Daddy's Section

<u>Why I Write</u>

Love Shared, Love Broken, Love Gone:

I wrote **Love Shared, Love Broken, Love Gone** because it was my point of view of what happened with my parents. How they liked, loved, envied and hated each other. I think that if my pops were not trying to be like the others, he looked up to, then he would've been satisfied with what he had instead of trying to be Mr. "Playa Playa." I also think that if my mama weren't so bent on getting even by getting hers too, then she would've realized that if she wasn't happy, there were better ways of going about it no matter what the family thought about the situation. I'm glad that they were able to love each other long enough to have my sister, my brother and me but I think they weren't the best as a pair and that's it.

Love Shared, Love Broken, Love Gone

Written For
Him and Her

He was a handsome youngin'
She was a beautiful somethin'
He was looking for a beautiful dummy
She was looking for an attractive honey

They meet

He thought she was beautiful and dumb enough
She thought he was handsome and a little tough
He thought, dumb enough not to suspect
She thought, a little tough to respect

They talk

He feels she could be the next big thing
She feels he can make her sing but not enough to
take a ring
He feels that he could get over the others
just for her
She feels that he is too much of a dog, who is
she to deter

They date

He cannot believe he found someone that can make
him feel this way

She cannot believe she still finds him more
exciting everyday

They are engaged

He thinks he has changed forever
She thinks she has learned never to say never

They're married with children

He sees she is not as she was before
She sees he is still looking for more whores

They were,
        They thought,
                They feel,
                        They cannot believe,
                                They think,
                                        They see
Do you want to know what
                                I was,
                        I thought,
                I feel,
        I cannot believe,
    I think,
I see

I speak

I was and am, the third offspring of the two
I thought the love shared would always be true
    I feel they were too young for a change
this big
I cannot believe, they were in so deep in that
hole without a shovel to dig
    I think they planned to be happy forever
I see they did not prepare for whatever

They cheated

He was not satisfied with just one
     She was ready for another instead of having
none
So when she was home he would leave to see her
workmate
     So when he went out she would call to see
if he was going to be late

They split

     He "knew" that she would always be his baby
She knew she would never go back to being his
lady

I speak out

I say, they spent too much time messing with each
other
     Then to think of what they could be to one
another
I say, he forgot about being a good father
     And she forgot about us being bothered
I say, those two together, were on the wrong
course
     Headed down that one-way street to divorce
He got remarried to her used-to-be workmate, as
suspected
     Hoping she would be affected
But what was not expected

     Was that she could care less.

Why I Write

His Words:

I wrote **His Words** because most people that are close to me don't know both sides of my daddy. They couldn't see why I felt like I hated him growing up. So I wanted to write something that explains his fun side, the side everyone else sees and the bad side, the side my siblings and I know very well. And I feel that this doesn't even get to the deepest root of how scary he can be, this is just the beginning of his rage.

His Words

Written For
The Speaker

When he's happy

His words are so calm
  as if it brought new life with every word
His words are soft
  but loud enough to hear the point
His words are meant to be
  heard not listened to, forgotten not remembered
  and laughed at not feared
His words are jokes
  to a very serious life
These words are always funny

  But when he's slightly angered

His words seem violent
  as if death follows every word
His words are heavy
  but clear for you to hear every detail described
His words are meant to be
  listened to not just heard, believed not
  ignored and feared not laughed at
His words are serious
  to a humorous life
His words are always mean

  See the difference?

<u>Why I Write</u>

Sugar Daddy:

I wrote **<u>Sugar Daddy</u>** because I thought my pops was trying to buy my love. First off, I wasn't wanted by him and when I was growing up I was really close to my mama, I still am and even though he and I are closer than we were, growing up with him around was hard for me. But then they got separated and eventually divorced and that only made me and my moms relationship better and his and I worse. I know that it's the parent's job to get their children prepared for the world, but I felt he was going to the extreme with me. I believe it was because he was jealous of what I had with my mama but I don't know for sure cause we don't talk like that and I don't know if we ever will. But at least after reading this book, he will know how I felt.

Sugar Daddy

Written For
The Uncommunicative

I'll give you a place to stay
I want to help pave the way
If it's a car you need
If it'll help you succeed
I got you
I'll even pay your way through school
Cause I see the life, you are trying to find
And your insurance, you know I don't mind
I'll buy you food
Only if I'm not rude
Whatever you need, it's my pleasure
Because you are my little treasure
And I want you to get you to get what you yearn
But I don't want to see you take; I want to help
you earn

The way this man talks to me
Not asking the important questions
Only trying to buy my love
So that I will stay
You wouldn't think that he was my daddy, more like
my sugar daddy.

<u>Why I Write</u>

Good Times:

I wrote **<u>Good Times</u>** because I wanted people and my dad to know that I know that it isn't always about the arguments between us and how I think that most times we talk, I feel like disrespect is the primary goal. So I just jotted down a few times to show that we have a good time with each other too. It took me a long time to write that little bit, cause I kept forgetting to make a record of those moments and when it came time to write it down, I would forget what happened, but I hope he likes it.

Good Times

Written To
Show There Are
Good Times

He let me and my brother move back in, today
He allowed me to stay even after the frustrations
of me being here
He made me laugh, today
He bought something that I didn't need but wanted
today
He took me all the way from the airport area
(where we live) all the way to Concord Mills (the
mall) after working a 10-hour shift, so that I
could buy my dress for my cousin's wedding
He made me laugh again
Today he bought me food without fussing that I
wasn't able to buy it myself
He didn't say anything about my mama after I
mentioned something about her
Today he made a plan with my sister to help my
brother, and I get to where we needed to be so
we could move out
Today he said he would assist my brother with
getting his car fix
Today he gave me the surprise of my life so far;
he bought me a laptop for Christmas
Today he hugged me and told me he loved me
Good times.

Even though we get into a lot of arguments because we are so much alike and aren't willing to back down when we feel disrespected, there are times that we share that I consider good moments. These are just a few, scattered and written down when I remembered to write them down which as you can see is not often.

Sister's Section

<u>Why I Write</u>

Sister's Poem:

I wrote **<u>Sister's Poem</u>** because sometimes I don't know my own "strength" word-wise, I tend to say things that may be harsh for a laugh. Now even though I get that laugh, unless it is brought up to me, I'm not thinking about the person I'm talking about or their feelings. There are a lot of sensitive people in my family, me being 1 of them, so I wrote this because some of the comments I made about my sister jokingly, someone told me that it wasn't funny, so this was my response.

Sister's Poem

Written For
My Sister

You are my sister, my favorite sister/cousin
PSYCH!!
You are a good friend, despite what you may think
and so I have written this poem from
the heart so here goes

When I talk about your weight, it's because I'm
jealous
I don't really like being this small, having no
curves and being all tall and lanky
When I talk about your smell after a hard working
day, it's because I'm jealous
I mean it's not that I want to smell like sweat
or anything, but it's the fact that I know you've
gotten up to do something with your day while I
lay in my bed watching T.V.
When I talk about your relationship with our
aunt, it's because I'm jealous of it
I wish I had that kind of support from one of my
aunts or anybody; I think it's cool
When I talk about YOU period, it's because
sometimes I wish I was you
But since I can't be you and can only be me
The only way I can show you, love, in other ways
than to tell you without laughing after, is to
pick on the ways that I look up to you

I love you, and that will never change I don't
like hurting your feeling but if I do, tell me,
and I'll NEVER say it again

P R O M I S E.

Why I Write

Remember Me:

I wrote **Remember Me**, in memory of my sister's fiance Kerry Moses. He died in a car accident February 8, 2006, a sad day for many. Though we might have had our tiffs, I liked him cause my sister loved him and he loved her and, that's a hard thing to do sometimes because she's not the easiest person to be around. He put up with her strong personality, and he fit in with the family cause he was friends with them before he even met my sister so that was a plus. I just felt like something had to be written to lift spirits and keep him in our memories. Also I think he would've loved it.

R.I.P.
Kerry Paul Moses
November 30, 1979 – February 8, 2006

Remember Me

Written For
The Memory Of Kerry Paul Moses
11/30/79 - 2/8/06

Even though I'm not here in the flesh, I am here
in spirit
There were too many memories shared for you to
ever forget
But I appreciate the tears
And there's nothing that you should ever fear
Cause I'm always near
I'm with you when you walk
And if ever you need to talk
Don't put your head down and cry
But lift it up to the sky
Say what you have to say
Then bow your head down and pray
That I am and you will be okay
Cause life is too short for all the fuss and
bother
So please don't worry, for I am with our Father
And you will get past this, once you see that I
am just as I should be
Cause I have finished my life's physical journey
And life will get back to the way it was before
Only I will be around each and every one of you
much more
Around my boys when they hang out
Around my brother when he feels doubt
Next to my girl when she falls asleep at night

Right there with my mom when she needs to know
everything is alright
I will be with my dad when he needs me
And with the rest of my own and extended family
I know that our time together was shorter than
planned
But things like this happen for a reason, so keep
trust in His hands
Cause I was taken to change someone, or something
Please don't let my life and death pass by for
nothing
If you don't know who the change was supposed to
affect, then everybody should shift something
At least I will see you cared for me as I cared
for you
And would do anything for me just as I would have
if I had to
Now in the words of my boy Dave Chappelle, it's
time for me to "Wrap It Up"
I hear the music playing and I see y'all tipping
your cups
But I will leave you with these words of
encouragement to keep on living
Cause even though God has taken, believe He will
keep on giving
So carry me in your thoughts cause I loved you
And anytime you need me, remember I am right
above you.

Brother's Section

<u>Why I Write</u>

Out On A L.E.M.:

I wrote **Out On A L.E.M.** because sometimes my brother hurts my feelings with the way he treats me and I wanted to bring this to his attention. It may be karma for how I do the same thing to other people, but I don't know I'm doing that, he does. The idea is that we are so close that I know we are bound to get on each others nerves but he crosses the line often, and that's all I'm saying. I have already said that I'm sensitive.

Out On A L.E.M.

Written For
My Brother

He's one that I admire

> He seems friendly to others, but to
> me he's fire

I know that he loves me to death

> And cares that I'm safe and in good
> health

But he doesn't show it, at least not to me

> I mean we laugh and play, but he
> gets mad so easily

And when his anger comes for me that day

> I'm ready to be insulted in that
> unique way

But you see, since I've known him all my life

> I know what will upset him and
> cause a strife

So the sadness I feel when he's mad is my fault

It's just how I am, it's what I was taught

You see I learned it all from him

His light shined so brightly on me but, now it's gone dim

So he shouldn't be mad at me cause he once did the same to the oldest

To me, he's like an angel in disguise acting as the boldest

Trying to be the strongest of all

Acting like he doesn't make mistakes like he can't fall

I'm sorry about the things I do to make him mad

But I want to know, is he, for making me sad

With the words that he uses to bring the pain

Makes me feel like my life is going down the drain

Along with a lot of drama

It's not my fault that I think he is the closest thing I have to our mama

I mean he looks just like her and makes me laugh
how she can

> But then anger begins to play too and
> I realize and begin to understand

That I love him for being himself, for real

> And I'm going to give him his time
> to heal

For all my faults and all of my mistakes

> Cause I'm out on a L.E.M.
> giving it all it takes.

<u>Why I Write</u>

Why This:

I wrote **<u>Why This</u>** because after my brother got in a car accident, I wanted to know why? I mean, everyone keeps telling me that things happen for a reason, so I just wanted to know what the cause was. This poem was my first one ever, and it was to question God's purpose of putting my brother in an accident, what was I thinking? It was just that, his accident was so horrible, and this guy never wore his seat belt but his seat belt saved his life. That's crazy to me, but I genuinely appreciate everybody that helped him that day including God, cause without Him my brother wouldn't be here. I know that now and I'll never doubt You again.

<u>Why This</u>

Written For
My Brother

I can't forget what happened
to my big and only brother
it was a tragedy, and I'm glad
that he is alright
but I still don't know why it
had to happen to him.
His face keeps showing up in my mind
even though he may be sitting right next to me
it makes me want to cry.
What if he was hurt more than he was?
I won't even think like that.
Almost every day that I went to school
and heard someone talking about it
I started to cry.
What if this would never have
happened, would our
life still be the same as it was?
About two weeks before the accident
my brother, his best friend
and I were talking about God
making things happen for
a reason but that gets me every time
because I can't seem to think what was the
reason for this?
Someday I will know the answer to that
I Hope!

Family & Friends Section

55

<u>Why I Write</u>

Better Treatment: Friends/Family:

I wrote **Better Treatment: Friends/ Family** because back in school I wasn't that popular, probably shouldn't even say that. But I went to middle and high school with my closest cousins D, and J. Now when it was summer the 4 of us, including my brother, were thick as thieves but as soon as school started, I was invisible to J who was in my grade. It seemed like her friends were more important than me. Okay, say we were in the middle of a conversation that she seemed to be into but as soon as one of her friends came up with something to say, it was like I was a chameleon, I just blended into the background. I know it wasn't intentional, but it hurt me back then. I guess writing this was just my way of venting and it helped me get over it, and we're cool now, not as close but cool.

Better Treatment: Friends/Family

Written For
A Cousin

She was thought of as a favorite in my eyes
I admired her but as we grew older, it just died down
Because she turned into someone totally different
Than what I expected for her
Teenage years was the turning point
Before, I thought that she was the nicest and funniest
Now, when she feels bored, on to the next
Right in the middle of your conversation
Because she was known by everyone
I think that's what it was based on, popularity
She only wanted to hear from others who were known
But I was semi-known I guess that wasn't enough for her
Because I kept getting interrupted
And she never ever heard all that I had to say
But I didn't start getting tired of it until our high school years
You see, I saw how I was SUPPOSED to be treated
And how I WAS being treated
By family none-the-less
And you know that ain't even right, at least in my eyes
But I never talked to her about this

I'd just walk away
To find someone who saw me and wanted me to talk
to them first before anyone else
I mean it was like I just turned into the wall,
like camouflaging
Right in front of her eyes and there was no need
to turn back if nothing's there
Now I wasn't jealous of her being popular
I think that's what she'll always be
I just thought that after God and yourself,
family was most important
But she will never hear this, at least not from me
Because I want to be the bigger person and not
cause drama
If she doesn't know, then she'll never know
Unless she finds this somehow or gets the same
treatment
But even then, I think it'll be too late to
apologize, for me...

<u>Why I Write</u>

You, You and You:

I wrote **<u>You, You and You</u>** because there was a situation that I went through that involved a guy I liked and a person that was close to me. They more than hooked up, someone told me, after them both knowing how I felt about the guy. But now that I have gotten past all that, I see now that with the help of God, they saved me from a world of hurt and for that, I thank Him, her and him.

You, You and You

Written For
Whoever Can Relate

You were the one who was more mature and got things done
Surpassed with ambition
Thought your looks would take left and right hooks
And beat up the competition
Couldn't be in the presence of dummies like it was a sin
Had to feel the energy of intuition

And you were like a closed door of everything I've tried reaching for
The prince charming in my play
Then you became the hoe that I didn't want any mo'
But every time you came around, I wanted you to stay
Just a favorite toy at the moment to give a bit of joy
Now you're the one I see right through like an x-ray

But you never let me lose sight of who was really in the spotlight
Helped me stay focused on me
Showed me that the hoe wanted those looks that fought with hooks
Something that I could never be

And that made me realize the lies told by loves
cries
Took the blindfold down so I could see

Without the more mature one, I would be with
the hoe
Thank you for helping me grow
Without the hoe, I wouldn't have felt the pain
Thank you for helping me walk through the rain
Without the guidance of sight, I would still be
living that life
Thank you for helping me get through without
strife.

<u>Why I Write</u>

Why I Pray:

I wrote **<u>Why I Pray</u>** because I love all of my family and the way they make me feel. If they were to change, then I wouldn't know what to do with myself. I believe I would be happy either way, but it would be a significant change to call normal. So I wrote this to let some of them know that I pray for them and love the people they are.

Why I Pray

Written For
Everyone

My mom is the sweetest person that I know I'll ever meet, she doesn't give me everything I want, but she finds the best way to tell me no even when she's angry.

My dad is a hilarious man and every joke he tells even when I don't get it at first there's always something in it that makes me tear up from all the laughing so when I finally get the joke all heck breaks loose.

My brother is the coolest prettiest heterosexual boy I have ever seen, and I love it when he comes to me about something he's wearing, what he smells like or how his shape up is.

My sister has some excellent dance moves even when she's playing around, and when I see it, I act like I don't like it but then I walk off and do it when I'm by myself.

My stepmom is easy to get, like on a joke or just hiding around the corner and saying "BOO!!!"

My stepsister has a real anxious sense of buying things with coupons and because of that, I always know what to get her for Christmas, gift cards.

My little niece has the sweetest little smile and the cutest little face but she is the most "active" little girl I know, and when you look at her from behind, she looks like Chucky, especially when she's kicking.

And all my grandparents make me happy in different ways but what they all have in common is the way they make me feel.

These are not all but a few people that I pray for every night, and I pray that they stay these ways because that's when I'm the most elated, and I see that they are happy too.

Why I Write

I wrote **I Am A Bacote** because I've always been told that I wasn't a Bacote, which is my mama's maiden name because that is not my last name. So I wrote this poem to say that I am proud to be who I am, but I am still a Bacote. Plus I was asked to write something for my family reunion.

I Am A Bacote

Written For
The Celebration Of My Family

I don't have my grandpa's height
Cause I am 5'9
I don't have my granny's good hair
And without a perm, you would see that
I don't have my aunts curves
Cause I'm just a skinny little thing
I don't have my uncle's strength
Nope, no muscle here
I don't have my cousin's maturity
Cause I'll crack a joke in a heartbeat
I don't have my brother's complexion
Cause, I am light skinned
I don't have my sister's anger
Cause life is too short for that
And I don't have my mama's maiden name
But I am a Bacote cause...
I do have
My grandpa's blood
My granny's tomboy-ness
My aunt's silliness
My uncle's compassion
My cousin's closeness
My brother's knowledge
My sister's protection
My mama's love
And for those reasons alone,
I am a Bacote.

<u>Why I Write</u>

What Do You Think It Should Be Called?:

I wrote **<u>What Do You Think It Should Be Called?</u>** Because as I have written before, I am a little harsh on people without knowing. So I wanted to apologize for it, sincerely.

What Do You Think It Should Be Called?

Written For
Those I Hurt

I'm sorry.

<u>Why I Write</u>

Strength (I'm Not Me, Without You):

I wrote **<u>Strength (I'm Not Me, Without You)</u>** because I love my family. I honestly don't know where I would be without each one of them. That's how close we are, so when I loss my granny (my dad's mom) January 14, 2014, randomly, it was a shock. I mean, my granny was a strong lady, she survived like 56 years of having type 1 diabetes, and she beat breast cancers ass, then it seemed like she died from the flu or something. I had just seen her the night before, and as I look back on that day, I regret not saying I loved her but I didn't think that was going to happen.

Then I loss my grandpa (my mama's dad) 4 days later, on January 18, 2014. It was the day we buried my granny, we got home, and I received a phone call from my mama, telling me that my grandpa had passed away.
Like how does this happen?
We knew something was wrong with him, but we didn't think he was as sick as he was. He hid it for a while, not even my granny knew, and everyone was hopeful that he would pull through. Only my grandpa and his doctor knew otherwise, I mean, I could tell too but ignored it, because my grandpa was a strong man, he was so sweet and funny but when he cried, saying to my cousin and me that he loved us, I knew it was more severe than anyone of us thought.
That was the last time I saw him alive.

I wrote the poem in honor of those two beautiful people. I felt a part of me died when I lost them, I know the whole family did but I'm happy that they are no longer suffering. Plus, I know they are looking down on all of us and we're making them proud everyday.

Strength
(I'm Not Me, Without You)

Written For
Those I Miss

Without you, I lose my feeling
Without you, I lose my grip
Without you, I lose my power
Cause within you I find my strength

Without you, I lose my foundation
Without you, I lose my installation
Without you, I lose my structure
Cause within you I find my character

Without you, I lose my stability
Without you, I lose my support
Without you, I lose my security
Cause within you I find my balance

Without you, I lose my willpower
Without you, I lose my ambition
Without you, I lose my motivation
Cause within you I find my drive

Without you, I lose my sound
Without you, I lose my melody
Without you, I lose my breath
Cause within you I find my voice

Without you, I lose my mind

Without you, I lose my individuality
Without you, I lose my heart
Cause within you I find me.

R.I.Paridise (Granny) Mamie L. Mauney
September 4, 1932-January 14, 2014

R.I.Paradise (Grandpa) Willie J. Bacote
January 2, 1932-January 18, 2014

Inspirational Section

<u>Why I Write</u>

When Killing Is Good and Bad:

I wrote **<u>When Killing Is Good and Bad</u>** because I don't understand how anyone can think that killing someone could ever be a good thing. I don't care where it goes down, what the person or people have done to others to get them in that situation, death is death, and I feel that if you're the one killing, then you are the murderer. I know that I might get a lot of hate or comments about this one but, this is my opinion on the subject.

When Killing Is
<u>Good and Bad</u>

Written For
Those Who Feel It

Trembling fingers, stumbling feet, fast beating heart
Scared to death of what is about to happen next
Shaky legs, weak arms, tears filled in eyes
As you pull the trigger and kill an enemy
Watery mouth, sweaty palms, skin feeling itchy
Walking in a war that you can't escape

Sturdy and heavy, big and black, powerful
Held close and tight like a newborn baby
Cocked and aimed, full and loaded, deadly
Hard and real, straight and narrow, harmful
Only pain can come from it on both sides of it

Rage, madness, not thinking
Before killing happens
Sinful, morning, can't stop thinking
After it all goes down

When this war happens in the streets, people get arrested and sentenced to prison life and are from then on out considered "CRIMINALS"
When this happens by the law or overseas or is ordered by The White House, people get rewarded

and sentenced to a better life and are considered
to be "HEROS"

Do I have to ask, what's really going on?
Killing should never be right, it will always be
wrong until the day we die.

Why I Write

Scared 2 Life (Part 1):

I wrote **Scared 2 Life** **(Part 1)** because its crazy to think about the many ways to die. I mean, you can drown, suffocate, burn, have a heart attack, get cancer or HIV/AIDS. For some reason I used to dream about dying, and when I would wake up I would forever think about the dream and that would make me not want to be around anything that could kill me, like electrical outlets or even while taking a shower, not wanting to put water on my face in fear of drowning. I always knew, but now I realize that God controls all of that and whichever way He decides for you to go, then that's how you're going to go but before I realized that, this is how I felt.

Scared 2 Life
(Part 1)

Written For
Those Who Feel It

My mama always used to tell me that if it's God's way, then things will be and not to live in fear because God doesn't live in fear. Now she told me that a lot because, I mean I know God knows everything that will go down but I don't and that scares the crap out of me and because of that it's like I expect the worst to happen, like death. So here's my thoughts on it.

I don't <u>drive</u>, partly because the thought of being responsible or partially responsible for someone's life while I'm behind the wheel creeps me out.

I don't <u>swim</u>, because I don't know how but lets say I learn one day and start thinking that I'm good enough to show off, mess around and start drowning around people that can't swim themselves, who's going to save me then.

I don't like to mess with <u>fire</u>, because I don't want to burn someone's house down doing something as simple as putting wood in the fireplace.

I don't be around real <u>guns</u>, because I don't want to be the target of someone playing around, thinking there aren't any bullets in it.

I don't like <u>people touching my neck</u>, because I don't like the feeling of not being able to breathe.

I don't play with <u>electrical outlets</u>, because I don't want something to happen and I get electrocuted.

I don't have <u>sex</u>, because nowadays people are not honest about their health when it comes to their sex life and I end up with HIV/AIDS or any other STD.

I don't <u>eat a lot of meat</u> but lots of vegetables, because I don't want the scare of a heart attack or stroke.

I don't <u>smoke</u> or try to be around smokers, because I don't want to go through life with a disease like cancer that can get operated on and seem like it's all gone then somehow it comes back

It's always been hard for me to <u>swallow pills</u>, so I try to relieve pain with the smallest medicines or not at all, and I also don't know the right dosage to take, so two is my maximum, even if it doesn't work.

These are not all but a few things that could kill me, some scary stuff.

<u>Why I Write</u>

Sometimes:

I wrote **<u>Sometimes</u>** because it was one of many poems that I wrote where I honestly felt inspirational. I wanted to talk about the spiritual world and how I sometimes hear and see things. Also when I wrote it, I guess I wanted to try to write something like how most poets wrote, this one and <u>Time</u>, thinking that my way probably wasn't the right way. However, I quickly learned that my style, telling stories with my writing was good enough.

Sometimes

Written For
Whoever Feels It

Sometimes I think I see angels
flying down the hall
Like a masterpiece painted on the wall
Where nothing is in a hurry and
everything is at a stall
While everyone who stands up falls
And babies that used to walk now crawl
When nothing seems short and everything tall
And no one is fighting, killing,
dying or living at all

Sometimes I hear voices at night
Where everything is clear but
nothing's in sight
When the things that seem significant in
the dark, are smaller in the light
While no one is lazy and everyone
has all their might
And does everything to win the fight
Because we are tired of doing things
separately, it's time to unite.

<u>Why I Write</u>

Time:

I wrote **Time** because I wanted to pay homage to God. He is so amazing and is always there, whether you believe in Him or not. He created us, He sacrificed His only son for us knowing that most of us would probably not appreciate it but He keeps on working around the clock, what better to compare Him to than time. It's there and it keeps going even when we're not thinking about it.

Time

Written For
Those Who Believe

Our time is like sight unseen
It's all that you can see and
everything in between
It passes you by, and you don't even know it
It's when you're sad, but you're
too afraid to show it

Our time is beautifully fast
It moves in your present, will go to your
future and has even been through your past
It flies through the blue sky
It can make you the happiest person
and still make you cry
It walks along with you when
you're feeling alone
It's there when you're little, and
it'll be there when you're grown

Our time is not our time at all
It's more like God being around when you call.

<u>Why I Write</u>

2nd Love Smoke:

I wrote **2nd Love Smoke** because there are a lot of people in my family and the world for that matter, that smoke. Usually, it's not even them getting sick from cancer or heart disease they inhale into their lungs but the people that are around and have to breathe the smoke that they're exhaling into the world. Secondhand smoke kills way more than someone sitting around smoking three packs a day. It's sad that most people know the risk of cigarettes but ignore the fact that it kills so many. So what I say to them is, if you want to smoke your life away fine, your choice but when it comes to the health of everyone else that doesn't then have some common courtesy.

2nd Love Smoke

Written For
The Smokers

Your 1st love isn't your girlfriend or boyfriend
Not your husband or wife
It might not even be your life
I don't think it's God either
And I can't clarify for sure
But not your family or friends neither
It's that small white round stick
That you seem to have to have quick
It's an addiction
That causes friction
Between you and us
And I know, because since you started back
You've been arguing about nothing, just to fuss
But it's something I want you to stop
So all the rest of your 2nd loves, me included,
won't just up and drop
Cause you are not just killing yourself
You're killing us too
And I'm not ready to see death
But if that's what it takes for you to stop
completely
Then I'm ready to sacrifice myself
To show everyone that this type of love can kill
as well

And no matter how you try to stop it, this love
won't fail
Cause once you inhale
That first breath of smoke
That's when I will be there to whisper in your
ears
Everything I just spoke
So that you will remember what used to be
How bad it was when the smokers killed me
And hopefully you will throw it down and walk
away
Then the next time it's offered, NO is what you
will say
On the 1st hand, it kills the 2nd handed
Just because you needed, the name branded
Pack of smokes
And I know it's not that easy to stop
But if it happens to you, remember what I just
wrote.

Why I Write

I:

I wrote **I** because I just felt like writing something down and that's what came out. Don't have an explanation for it, I mean I guess I wanted to show all the things I am and everything I can be.

1

Written For
Those Who Feel It

I am dependent
And I won't go to waste
I am a defendant
Let me plead my case
I am affection
You can see it all over my face
I am here for your protection
Help me save our race
I can be your blessing
Glue your life back together with God's paste
I'm just guessing
You're gonna need your space
I'm a passer
At a non-stop pace
I am a harasser
Oh, I'll give you a taste
I am a stalker
I'm right outside your place
I am a talker
My words will leave a trace.

<u>Why I Write</u>

We'll Find A Way:

I wrote **<u>We'll Find A Way</u>** because I thought it was tragic what happened to the (Hurricane) Katrina victims. It doesn't make sense that the government didn't see the reason to help on time but, I bet if that president could run again, Y'all would probably vote him back in. His actions angered me but very proud of the celebrities and everyone that stood up to help, so I wanted to write something to show that you (the critical people that run the world) can leave us in the deepest darkest hole but when we come together, we will find a way out.

We'll Find
A Way

Written For
Victims of Hurricane Katrina

Why the hell don't you care
How can people be so unfair
Is it because you can't afford to lose the rich
white
Or does the poor, which are mostly black, have to
fight more out of spite
How can you look at race and status and choose
who lives
Because when you wanted war, didn't we become
your shield
Why would you do this to Americans like you
Don't you see we need help too
Just because we're a little poor
Maybe that means we need a little more
What do you think, you're God or something
Get elected, give a little take a little and leave
us with nothing
It is true, right no need to pretend
I mean we cannot help how our life begins or ends
At least we know who our friends are
And I'm sure everyone appreciates the help from
the stars
All these people going through this
Separated from their family with no "I love you,"
no hug and no kiss
Lives are being lost

Because you ain't willing to pay the cost
And look how the people are working together
I guess you should stop saying "never"
Cause the more you push us off on one another
The more we find a way to help each other
So you keep being your selfish self
Just know that one day you will need our help
And we will be there cause a million, let alone two wrongs...
You know the saying, and it will only keep us strong
Just remember life lives and death dies
What happens in between determines whether you'll make it past the blue skies
There will be no room for tears when you're burning
I am just saying, this might be your final warning.

Why I Write

Help B.U.M.S. (Before yoU and Me Suffer):

I wrote **<u>Help B.U.M.S. (Before yoU and Me Suffer)</u>** because I feel like all homeless people get a bad rep because of the few that fake it or abuse the fact of others helping them. So I thought it was time to take a closer look at what could have happened to the people that may feel like less than they should cause of how society treats them.

Help B.U.M.S.
(Before yoU and Me Suffer)

Written For
Those Who Feel It

I know that on the surface all you see
Is this pathetic waste of a person that I
call me
With a jacket two sizes too small
A wife beater 4 sizes too tall
And some corduroys on in the 90-degree weather
Just somebody that you think could do so much
better
And even though I hold a sign that says "will
work for food..."
You think that translates to "give me money so
I can go buy booze"
But if you took time out to get to know me,
this is what you would find
I'm a father to 3 kids that may or may not be
mine
Cause while I was overseas fighting in Bush's war
The fact that I wasn't here, made my wife not
love me anymore
So she cheated with Will, my best friend of too
many years
A friend that I thought would never do this
even after a night full of beers
And when the letter came to the base a week
after I had to leave

I laughed cause I thought it was another trick
up their sleeves
But when the letters stopped coming, I knew it
was real
Then 2 months before I was about to be honorably
discharged, I got a letter from Will
Saying it was just that one time and he's sorry
for all the pain caused
But reading the next part is what made my
heartbeats pause
Cause I learned that my wife was now pregnant
with my triplets and that he was walking away
Seems to me he shouldn't have been there in
the 1st place
So now I'm a soldier that came home to so much
hurt
And an ex-husband to a woman that has done so
much dirt
But no matter what any test says, I've been in
those kids lives since the day they were born
All my army money goes to them and I keep your
unneeded coins
So I really do need food, just as the sign reads
And don't be so quick to judge people and the
lives they lead
Cause you could be me, begging for help
And I could be the one deciding whether or not
to share my wealth.

Why I Write

Blind Date:

I wrote **Blind Date** because I was tired of what my cousins were doing to me. It's like they didn't care about me possibly finding something real, that's why when their guy friend, who was beautiful, had a friend and I'm called in for the friendly but ugliest guys ever. So I wrote this to bring to their attention that I don't want to take one for the team anymore.

Blind Date

Written For
The Set Uppers

Now I like tall, light-skinned, toned, humorous,
ambitious men
Toned to the point of him getting down to do
push-ups and doing more than 10
And I've been set up to meet many dudes with
strong ambitions
But they don't seem to fit the rest of my descriptions
So because of that I'm told that I think I'm too
good
No, I know what I want and I think that should
be understood
At least by people that know me and try to set
me up all the time
And when we meet, the dudes say I'm fine
Well I don't know about that, I believe I'm cute
I mean I'm a regular chick with a tomboy/girly
style and everywhere I go I rock Timberland boots
Man I feel like I'm going crazy
That's why if I can, I try to put my limit of
alcohol in my system so everything will be hazy
And they know that the dudes they pick out don't
look right for me
That's why I ask for a photo when even they
haven't seen how he'll be
Now do I sound like a person that thinks her shit
don't stink
Answer me, I really want to know what y'all think

This is one of my biggest problems, fuck it, this
is my only big problem
And I know there is someone out there who can
help me solve it
Am I right, I mean there is someone for all of us
Shit man... excuse me, I don't mean to cuss
But I can't help it, I just want to wake up and
have that man in my sights
However I keep going through all the wrongs
before my Mr. Right
And most of the time I'm just there for support
But if it were my way, after I saw the ugliness,
I would pause the scene and abort
Now if that makes me sound conceited
Them maybe I got a reason
Maybe this is how it's suppose to be, some sign
of fate
Well that's what I get for going on a blind date.

<u>Why I Write</u>

Scared 2 Life Part 2:

I wrote **<u>Scared 2 Life</u> <u>Part 2</u>** because I still felt like saying something about the things we do and the fact that if we just let God in He will be that support we might need to help us change our minds. He's always there, all we have to do is accept Him into our lives.

Scared 2 Life
Part 2

Written For
Those Who Feel It

I am the hand that holds the gun
I am the arms that are tired of stroking the water
I am the finger that lights the match
I am the right foot that pressed the gas to speed up the car
I am the mouth full of pills
I am the neck in the rope
I am the vein popping out the arm
I am death

He is the mind that tells me to put it down
He is the strength that pushed me to keep stroking
He is the mouth that blows the breath to put out the light
He is the left foot or hand that pushes or pulls the emergency brake
He is the tongue that pushes the pills out of me
He is the knife that cuts the rope
He is the hand that lets go of the belt
He is life.

<u>Why I Write</u>

Inside and Out (redone)

I wrote **Inside and Out (redone)** because I was tired of guys trying to make me change my mind on the things I want and am asking for when it came to finding somebody to date. Okay, say I'm on a dating website, they ask you to describe yourself and then to describe what you're looking for... so when I write down what I'm looking for, why are you trying to make me change my mind? Just cause you like the way I look or how I may seem after reading my profile, doesn't mean that we will make the perfect fit. I mean, it's a two way-street and naturally if you don't fit what I'm asking for then that guarantees that this world doesn't want us together. Sorry, I don't try to be mean but I know what I want and it'll only change if what I am attracted to changes.

Inside and Out

Written For
Those Who Feel It

I know that beauty is only skin deep
But until you know the person, the outside is
what makes you want to take that leap
It keeps
You interested until you realize who that person is
Then you can determine whether you and that
person will live in extreme and total bliss
This
Outside beauty can only take you so far
But it is the inside that may or may not lift you
to the stars
Wars
Between you and your feelings
If you're willing
To keep dealing
With the fact
That you are who you are and no one can change
that
And after explaining yourself a million and one
times, don't be afraid to turn your back
Cause no matter how hard they try to change your
mind, you can't help that you have a preference
And the difference
Between you and them, is that you know what will
and will not spark your interest
You're not just out there trying to get something
from the first person you see
For me

I know exactly what I want that person to be
And trying to fight it
Is pointless, cause God made things the way they
are and ain't no way you can rewrite it
So for everyone out there who are undecided
Keep your heads up, is all I can say
Cause today
I can't help what I like but that's how it's gonna
stay.

<u>Why I Write</u>

Choices:

I wrote **Choices** because someone very close to me got sick and it wasn't their fault, but I felt a need to bring awareness to not necessarily the person but to the sickness. I love this person and in no way am I writing this to make you feel away, I want people to think about their choices. To make it like, if I were to do this, would I be considered this. I like this poem, I have more to add to it, but for now, this is what I have.

Choices

Written For
Those Who Can Relate

If I have unprotected sex with someone that has
AIDS,
Am I committing suicide?

And if that person knows he has it but doesn't
say anything and does it anyway,
Is he a murderer?

If my mother tells me to give her money and I
know this money is for bad things,
Am I disobeying her by telling her no?

And if I say yes,
Am I supporting her habit?

If I break-up with a man who said he was single
but I found out he was married,
Was I an adulterer?

If I got raped and did not report it,
Am I an accomplice to him doing it again?

But if I did report it,
Am I a snitch?

And if I got pregnant from that rape and had an
abortion,
Am I playing God?

If I pine for love that will never be,
Am I living?

If I have an emotional relationship with a man
who is not my husband,
Am I cheating?

If I can see myself fulfilling all my goals,
Am I a psychic?

And if I want to see a world where none of the
bad in this poem happens,
Am I dreaming?

<u>Why I Write</u>

Etc.:

I wrote **<u>Etc.</u>** because I wanted to write down the possibilities of how I see my life going if I decide to put myself in these situations. Also, how I feel about marriage because of how some things happened in some parts of my family. I don't know if it'll eventually be the reason for me not to get married but so far, I feel that if I'm going to end up alone anyway then whats the point?

Etc.

Written For
Those Who Feel It

Dating-
You want to take me out; you want to call me every night, you want to have me all to yourself, et cetera

Relationship-
You love me; you'll be there for me, you'll never cheat, et cetera

Marriage-
We'll have a house, we'll have the white picket fence, we'll have the big tree with the tire swing, et cetera

Family-
You'll stay with me during the pregnancies; you'll tell the kids bedtime stories, you'll help them with their homework, et cetera

The Problems-
You won't hit me again; you won't cheat again, you'll be the man you were at the beginning, et cetera

Divorce-
You'll let me keep the kids; you'll take care of their needs, we can keep everything, et cetera

<u>What Really Happened-</u>

He did take me out, he did call me every night, and he did have me all to his self

He did love me, he was there for me, and he didn't cheat

We did have the house, the white picket fence and the tree with the tire swing

He did stay with me during the pregnancies, he did tell the kids bedtime stories, and helped them with their homework

He did hit me again, he did cheat again and never was the man he was at the beginning

We went through an evil custody battle for the kids, and he did take care of their needs when they were with him, and we kept nothing

Et cetera, et cetera, et cetera, et cetera, et cetera, et cetera.

Why I Write

Power To The People:

I wrote **Power To The People** because I felt it was time to give props to all the people that put up with the stress and dumbness of what goes on in the world. There are a lot of haters in the world, and they don't care what they say or who they hurt, so I wanted to say that you all who get hated on and keep going on with your lives are heroes to me.

Power To The People

Written For
The People

Power to the people
For all the hard work
And putting up with the jerks
For not complaining about not getting the perks
For getting called less than dirt
But learning how not to show how much your feelings were hurt
For filing sexual harassment when it was more than a flirt
And when someone put their hand up your shirt

Power to the people
For getting back up when they pushed you down
Not knowing how to swim but getting up the strength not to drown
Or the courage not to go downtown
And getting fired and leaving with a smile instead of a frown
And in a boring party acting like a clown

Power to the people
For being strong and black
And never looking back
And being the rose that grew from the crack
Also for putting your fist up at the track
For believing that you could beat the slack

And power to the people

Because I am apart of you
Because I believe too
In all the things we can do
And I will forever be stuck to my people like
glue.

Why I Write

Know It Well:

I wrote **Know It Well** because there is no alcohol abuse in my family but it is something that I can say is a big part of our lives. Because we are so close to my mama's side, we love to have fun with each other whether that be partying or just hanging out and alcohol is usually apart of that. But what would happen if you took one drink too many...?

Know It Well

Written For
Those Who Feel It

You know when you are at a party, and you are dancing all crazy on the table and on everyone you see?
It's called alcohol
You know when you get mad and start screaming and yelling at whoever is around you, for absolutely no reason?
It's called alcohol
You know when your family and friends keep telling you to "slow down" or "take it easy"?
It's called alcohol
You know when you're swerving while driving and are all over the road?
It's called alcohol
You know when the highlight of your life is when you and your friends are competing on who can burp the loudest?
It's called alcohol
You know when you stand up and quickly fall back down, but when you finally get your balance, you stagger on your first step?
It's called alcohol
You know when you wake up and the first thing you taste is throw-up?
It's called alcohol
You know when you wake up in your bed and you don't remember how you got there or why your clothes are ripped, and there is blood all around you?

That's called rape and alcohol
You know when you wake up in a jail cell after blacking out?
It's called alcohol
You know when you've woken up from a crazy night of partying that you don't remember and all you see on the T.V. is how this lady and her four-month-old baby was killed in a hit and run last night?
You know how you were thinking how sad that was and wondered how people could do something like that?
You know how you went out to the garage to get something from your car, you see that it was dented with hair and blood on it and you realize that you were that somebody?
That's called murder and alcohol
You know when you open your garage door and all you see is a whole bunch of cops surrounding you with their guns drawn?
That's called alcohol
And if you know anyone of these a little too well, then you should consider yourself an alcoholic.

Why I Write

Untitled:

I wrote **Untitled** because of pass incidents. Not necessarily me but people I have known in my past that went through verbal and physical abuse and because of those things, I feel I'll remember the signs before anything like that could ever happen to me. I know that sticking around during and after something like that happens, is your choice but I don't think I could ever stay. This poem is one of my favorites, and yet I still can't figure out what to call it, so untitled it shall be.

Untitled

Written For
The Abusers

So just wave your hand in the air
And bring it down to her face like you just don't
care
But turn the music up 'til it blares
Now do it faster and faster until all you see is
tears
And when you calm down watch her sit there
And watch her stare
Thinking why life isn't fair
While you wonder why she ain't sending up a flare
Or trying to call the mayor
To come save her from your evil lair
Cause even with prayer
It still has to be hard to bear
Then think about why you get so mad at the fact
of her changing her hair
Or the clothes she wears
And why when you get mad, you have to swear
Even when you know good enough well, this girl
is very rare
And apparently you're not looking to share
But one day she is going to realize that y'all
ain't the best as a pair
And all that's left is that one single chair
In front of the window, that she is sitting in
right now.

Why I Write

What I See:

I wrote **What I See** because my brother wanted to impress a girl and he knew I could write poetry so he asked me to write him something for her. But after I wrote it, he looked at me like "NO!!! that ain't what I wanted, I don't know the girl to be talking like this." So he scrapped it until I remembered that I wrote it. I don't know, someone might like it and will either smile or be inspired enough to get creative when trying to impress someone.

What I See

Written For
Those Who Feel It

I see stars sparkling all night

I see flowers blossoming in the sunlight

I see little kids pointing and
smiling when I pass

I see people living every day
like it's their last

I see the rainbow before the sky gets wet

I see a finished picture before the
painter has his colors set

I see paradise everywhere I look

I see "happily ever after" in every book

I see leaves turning beautiful
colors while walking by

I see all this with my own two eyes

I see pain quickly turned to pleasure

I see happiness being someone's treasure

I see love happening right
in front of my face

I see God working at a non-stop pace

And I wonder why when I'm
alone, none of this I see

It's because I'm missing the critical
factor and that's you being here

with me.

<u>Why I Write</u>

Power To The People (redone):

I wrote **Power To The People (redone)** because I felt that the other one was more about anybody that suffered something and I liked it, but I wanted to write something about the people that helped someone else and the things that happened that led us to have a black president. So I listed just a few crucial moments in our history, the influential people and hero's that played a massive part in our history, to now.

Power To The People
People
(redone)

Written For
The People

Power to the people *(Slavery Survivors)*
That knew it wasn't right
Being beat just because your skin wasn't white
Felt like giving up but stood up to fight
And was able to escape, so that the generations
to come could see the light

Power to the people *(Civil Right Movement)*
That had the guts to trust the King *(Dr. Martin Luther King Jr.)*
Who followed him to the "mountaintop" with
uplifting songs to sing
And believed in the ability to change things
With a non-violent approach, despite the punishment
that it might bring

Power to the people *(War, Police and Firefighting Hero's)*
That believed in the cause
Who was fighting for the survival of your country,
no need for an applause
Even though sometimes, your leader didn't have
the balls
You still were there to enforce the laws

Power to the people *(Hurricane Katrina Survivors)*

That knew how to survive
Who saw the "Man In Charge" was cool with letting you die
Though you didn't think you had to be a hero for yourself, you weren't afraid to try
That showed the ones involved, sometimes you can't just stand by

Power to the people *(President Barack Obama)*
That finally felt like it was time for a change
And saw promise in his campaign
Who was tired of looking at the world and being ashamed
It's time to celebrate with each other, lets pop the champagne

Power to the people *(Everyone)*
Who were no longer looking at the world through a peephole
And looked past the outside appearance of a person and found their deep soul
That was tired of acting like a bleep-hole
It's you, that makes me proud to be apart of the people.

Why I Write

Help B.U.M.S. (Before yoU and Me Suffer) 2:

I wrote **Help B.U.M.S. (Before yoU and Me Suffer) 2** because like I said before I wanted to make this a series but usually when I think of the possibilities that could have happened to lead a person to this life, I would get writer's block. Luckily I was able to pop this one out and hopefully more in the future, but for now, here you go...

Help B.U.M.S.
(Before yoU and Me Suffer) 2

Written For Awareness

I know that on the surface all you see
Is this pathetic waste of a person that I call me
With dirt on my face, clothes and all over my hands
And a smell that guarantees the flies will always come to me when they need a place to land
Also some hoochie mama shorts on and what looks like a Freddy Kruger sweater
Just someone that you think could do so much better
And even though I hold a sign that says "will work for food..."
You think that translates to "give me money for the drugs I use"
But if you would've just taken time to get to know me, this is what you could have seen
If you couldn't tell by my accent, I'm from New Orleans
Yes, my family and I were there when (Hurricane) Katrina hit
And I knew in order for us to survive that deadly water, I had to be strong and I couldn't quit
While sitting on our roof and watching the boats go by
Watching other people getting rescued, took the strength I had for my kids, right out of me and it made me cry

Now just cause we lived by the water didn't mean
we knew how to swim
So we thanked God the moment He sent us him
Mr. Williams, someone we would've never thought
A man from a family of which my family always
fought
If being racist was the thing to be, they would've
been Hitler and his troops in their truest form
But a saint he was to us that day after the storm
He could only fit 3 others besides him and Tom,
his brother
And we were HIS (Mr. Williams) choice, and even
if words were never exchanged, it was clear that
Tom didn't like the fact that his brother might
be a nigger lover
But in the midst of us being "saved" saved we
were sent to Texas
Which was great for my son and daughter cause
that's where my ex was
When I lost my job, my kids went to live with
their daddy and I ended up living by some train
tracks
Looking for anything that would help me get my
family back
So I really do need food just as the sign reads
And don't be so quick to judge people and the
life they lead
Cause you could be me, begging for help
And I could be the one deciding whether or not
to share my wealth.

Why I Write

Bully:

I wrote **Bully** because I wanted to bring more awareness to the fact that parents bully their kids too. It can either force their kids to bully other kids or push them somewhere worse. So this is a story about a person that's so out of control, and it's crazy cause he has no idea how out of control he is, to push one of the strongest people I know, to tears and to have suicidal thoughts. Plus it's happened to me, someone has driven me to consider ending it all but luckily our faith in God outweighed our faith in that person, and we didn't go through with it.

<u>Bully</u>

Written For
Awareness

He complained again,
He felt ashamed again,
He popped a vein again,
Got emotionally drained again
And he needed someone to blame again.

He wasn't as strong this time,
He saw the wrong this time,
He changed his tone this time,
Felt like he was alone this time
And he had nowhere to belong this time.

He doesn't like to talk, he only yells
He doesn't like to ask, he only tells
He doesn't like to move on, he only dwells
Anything to block the knowledge that he is the
only one to fail.

He doesn't like to listen, he only ignores
He doesn't like to show feelings, he only
stores
He doesn't like to interact in the
conversation, he knows it'll only lead to more
Anything to block the knowledge that he'll
never let anyone see his core.

He wasn't thinking,
Wasn't drinking,

He was so angry that he wasn't blinking
And while he felt like he was floating above the water,
The other guy was sinking.

He stopped trying,
Stopped lying,
He was so depressed that he started crying
And while the other guy was going on and on
about how he should be living,
He thought about dying.

His yelling for no reason was washed away with one beer
With sweat beads being wiped away until they disappeared
And that's when he realizes, the thought of him being a failure is what he really fears.

His hiding his true feelings inside start to wear thin
With tears running from his eyes down to his chin
And even though he didn't go through with it, that's when thoughts of how to kill himself begin.

He went on washing his car like what he said, was said the right way.

He wiped his tears and went on playing on his computer like he did every day.

Neither one of them ever spoke of what transpired, in fact I don't even think that the "bully" even knows what happened

as a result of his unneeded ranting. There
were no apologies made between the two, a
matter of fact they went out the next day
like nothing ever happened. But the real
sad part about this is that this <u>Father</u>
won't know anything about how he made his
<u>Son</u> feel that day until he reads this.
Such a shame.

My Section

Why I Write

What Is It About Me (Insecurity):

I wrote **What Is It About Me (Insecurity)** because I used to think that guys didn't like me because I was a tomboy, the clothes I wore or my appearance. So I figured that if I could, I would change for them, but then I realized that if I adjust for them, then who will I be? I would lose sight of me, to be something for someone else that won't love me as I will. What I'm saying is, you shouldn't change for anyone, to be you and when the right one comes he or she will love you for what you are not what you can be.

What Is It About
<u>Me</u>
<u>(Insecurity)</u>

Written For
Me and Everyone Like Me

It's my appearance
So I'll wear tighter clothes
It's my attitude
So I'll be the sweetest person
It's my hair
So I'll change it every day
It's my face
So I'll get plastic surgery
Why can't I get a guy to notice me?

It's my body
No curves = no man
It's the fact that I don't put out
No sex = no man
It's my personality
Too goofy = no man
So I'll change

I'll get fat then work out
I'll go out and have sex with every man I see
I'll be as determined as a girl can get
I'll change for them

But what about me?
What do I feel?

_ theshy1

I feel that I am beautiful inside and out
Who cares about what a man wants
I'm what's important...
                    To me.

<u>Why I Write</u>

This Girl, This Woman:

I wrote **This Girl, This Woman** because that's how I felt during my parent's separation and divorce. I wanted everyone to stop with all the hate and lies told, just because they didn't like each other anymore. Sometimes my thoughts went to the worst possible places, so I needed to get those out of my head, and this is where they went...

This Girl, This Woman

Written For
Those Who Know Me Best

This little girl loved her family so much
This little girl felt blessed for what she had
This little girl heard stories and started to lose trust
This little girl had to choose between her mom and dad

This girl loved her mother to death
This girl started forgetting her father
This girl would do anything to make sure her mama was in good health
This girl wondered about all the fuss and being bothered

This young woman left and missed her mom a lot
This young woman sees that to get by; she'll have to take her dads bad with the good
This young woman is learning to be thankful for what she's got
This young woman sees the blessing of no longer living in the hood

This woman will have everything spiritually, but she's going to lack that physical and emotional love

This woman will hate to watch her family live
their separate lives
This woman will talk to everyone still but is
going to wish she didn't have to look down on
them from above
This woman will hate the fact that during their
good times, they hated each other while she cried

This little girl was me
This girl was me
This young woman is me
This woman will be me if the
hate and lies don't stop.

<u>Why I Write</u>

That Day:

I wrote **<u>That Day</u>** because everybody around me keeps pestering me about me doing something with my life. Like a stable job, license, a boyfriend, etc. But I can't be forced into doing something especially if it benefits you, which is why some of the people were trying to push these things on me. I say that one day I will... but today is not that day.

That Day

Written For
Those Who Feel It

One day I will get off my lazy butt and do something with my life...
And one day I will stop procrastinating and get my license and a car...
But today is not that day

One day I'll get over you, go out and find someone who wants to be my friend first then my lover...
And one day I'll stop being afraid to fall in love and start listening to the advice given...
But today is not that day

One day I will learn how to be independent of myself and move out of my daddies house...
And one day I will stop depending on everyone else and learn to do things for myself...
But today is not that day

One day I will get over not wanting to buy my feminine products...
And one day I will learn that the world does not revolve around me...
But today is not that day

One day I will realize that everything I want I can have if I try...
And one day I'll go back to school to help me realize that...

But today is not that day

One day I will return to church and continue thanking God for being my one and only savior cause He is why I am still here...
And one day He will make everything clear,
Now that day is today.

Why I Write

My First:

I wrote **My First** because that's how I felt about the guy that I couldn't get over for a very long time and who was the inspiration for a lot of my poems. He is the reason for how I live my "love life" now; I'm scared but eager to have something that will last cause I never really had anything real. I will always remember what he taught me about what I need and won't settle for when it comes to love.

My First

Written For
You

You were my first
The one I gave it all to
I felt it when you burst
And I was who you called out to

I felt your everything
You pulled me in
To you, I wanted to cling
But that was then

Now we have changed
You say you avoided the crash
Something already arranged
But you burnt it to ash

I trusted you with it
I thought you would be the one
I saw how you were with it
And I saw you having fun

So I had to let you know
That I wanted to be more than just friends
Even if you were a ho
I was willing to let that blow in the wind

I fought for you
You were all I needed
I cried every night for you

Just never succeeded

I knew you were right
But I couldn't stop the feeling
I wanted to be the one in your sights
I wanted us together to start the healing

I tried to be blind
And let go of what I felt
And I tried to be kind
To something I thought would be my safe belt

It was never my fault
To feel that you were sent from above
And never in a million years, will I ever forget
the lessons taught
By my first love.

Why I Write

Written Soul:

I wrote **Written Soul** because I would often think about how his and my conversation should have gone and how it went. I wish I would've explained myself better so that he knew that I liked him, but I didn't know how to go about it after telling him. This poem is how I wished it was but even in these words written; I was afraid. That's why I couldn't quite get what I felt, out there, either.

Written Soul

Written For
You

How can I start this conversation
When the words needed seems so far away
There are a million thoughts passing, as the angels fly over us
My spirit, my soul speaks out
But no words pass through my lips
I can see this person I want to be, spilling my guts out to you
But nothing happens
It's like when you're in my sights; my heart breaks down
All that love pulsating through every beat, just tears it up
I know that no one can take the feelings from my heart,
Move them to my brain and force them out of my mouth
But I wish someone could translate my silence
Or sign my feelings to you
Because even though I believe in what this could be between us
I don't think I will be the one to start it,
You have to
I know that if you feel an ounce of what I'm saying
Then maybe your soul is my souls mate
And if not,
Then at least I will have gotten a chance to experience my souls dream
I love you.

<u>Why I Write</u>

When I Write:

I wrote **When I Write** because these are the things I think about when I write. My family, after God and me, are the most important people in my life. If only you knew them as I know them, you'd say who better to get my inspiration from.

When I Write

Written For
My Inspirations

I think about my mama changing her life for me
if she only knew how I felt
I think about her loving me for the rest of my
life
I think about how lucky I am to have her as my
mother
She inspires me to want to do something spectacular
to give her everything that she wanted to give
herself but couldn't because of my sister, brother
and I

I think about my daddy trying to be a better
person if he could only read how I feel
I think about him wanting to make his and my
relationship better
I think about him not caring so much, which
forces him to tear my mama down in front of me
just because of his jealousy of how close we are
He inspires me to want to be a better parent if
it is in my cards to be one and also to be a
better person

I think about my siblings, my brother showing his
love better than he does now
I think about him changing his ways when it comes
to him thinking he doesn't need anyone around him
He inspires me to be me and knowing the difference
between wanting to be by myself and being lonely

I think about my sister not being so angry about
everything
I think about that day when she will stop worrying
about what people think and say about her
I think about her forgetting about the negativity
around her and start living her life according
to God's plan
She inspires me to have fun when I can cause life
is way too short to be serious and angry all the
time

I think about the family that I have that pushes
me to be better no matter how stubborn I am
I think about repaying them for all the things
that they have done for me physically, emotionally
and mentally
I think about them not trying to change who I am
They inspire me to never stop dreaming cause if
I don't strive to be better, then I never will be
I think about the family that I have that believes
everything they do is better than anything I
could ever do
I think about them trying to bring me down when
they feel I'm dreaming too big
I think about how I hurt when one of them puts,
what I feel is my best, down
They inspire me to keep belief in myself cause I
might be the only one who trusts in my abilities

I think about my grandparents, M&L because they
want the best for me no matter what it is
I think about the J&W because they treat me
like an individual and they don't compare me to
anybody and I appreciate that

They inspire me to want to be able to lead a long and fulfilling life as they all have and also to keep family close

I think about me not being afraid to voice my opinion on things I don't like and everything I do
I think about being independent and paying back all my debts to the people who act like money is really significant

I think about me, for once, wanting to be ME!!

<u>Why I Write</u>

?'s:

I wrote **?'s** because, with all the crap I've been through with that guy, I had often wondered when and if I was ever going to get over him. So I wrote down some questions to look inside of me, and hopefully one day I would be able to answer.

<u>?'s</u>

Written For
Those Who Can Relate

Why doesn't he want me
How many years will I let go pass, knowing he'll
never be mine
Why do I yearn for him so much
I mean why him
Is he the one
Does he really know how I feel
Do we have a life together
When will I stop comparing others to him
Will I ever let him go
Can I call him and not be afraid to tell him my
feelings
Will he ever be so kind, to not hurt my feelings
again
Did I go about this the wrong way
Why hasn't he called me
At least to say hi
Where is he anyway
Am I wasting my time
Will I ever get these moments back
When will he feel about me the way I feel
about him
Why can't I see the signs
Why do I ignore the advice to leave him alone
Is my love for him going to ever end
Who will ever take his place
Is it my fault
What time is it

Has it been 30 minutes already
Or 19 years and a half hour
Should I stop now
Would y'all stop looking at me
He will be mine one day, right
Anybody got answers?

Why I Write

dExpressed Feelings:

I wrote **dExpressed Feelings** because sometimes I get so depressed to the point of thinking about what the world be like without me in it. I know I would never go through with it, but it always helps me to write stuff down, to get these feeling out of my head. So I wrote it down, so i could at least express them, and they're not all bottled up in my head. And again I will NEVER go through with this plan; I love my family, my life and God way too much to ever do something like this. I promise this is just a poem.

dExpressed Feelings

Just Written

I have lived too long and have gained absolutely nothing, so I feel my being here is a waste of time. I am ready to leave this physical place and live in the spiritual one. I am sorry if I have disappointed my family especially my mama, because I was always on her about her life and here I am about to end mine. I have realized that there is nothing here, I have not found my soul mate, I do not want to go to school, I cannot drive and I am very immature for my age. I know that all I have is my mama but if she does not care about how I feel when it comes to the life she leads, then I am ready to go. So goodbye to my mama, who taught me about God and His way and for the way she loved me until today, the day I will die, thank you. Goodbye to my father, who I did not have the best relationship with and even though we both wanted to change that, neither one of us ever did anything about the situation. Goodbye to my siblings, Brother my "Baby Bro". I loved you being my older and only brother even though we've had our share of incidents and moments that left us both hurting. Sister, you were my old and mean sister. Just kidding, you know you are in my heart but your attitude reminded me too much of daddies and you know how I felt about him. And F, my stepsister, you were more mature than all of us cause you were older and had been through things but I felt your connection to us.

I know that we didn't just get along because of the marriage between our parents, I did feel that you were uncomfortable with the whole thing as we all were but I hoped that we helped you feel more comfortable with it after time but I definitely say you helped me and I appreciated that. I don't think that I could have picked a better "step" family to be apart of, cause I had fun knowing all of you. C, you know how I felt about my mama, and I know that you were not trying to take her place, but you could have spoken up a little more especially when daddy was treating you so poorly. I wish that you would've shown more of your strong side when we needed to see it but I did appreciate and love you. And I knew that without you, there would be no F or T, which to me was one of the greatest gifts in my life, my 1st and only niece, so far. T, I loved you and I hope that if there is anything that you will remember me by, please don't let it be the way I chose to leave this world. Any bad situation that you may have please don't follow my lead, cause I am being a coward right now and I'm sorry. Everyone, please remember the good times you had with me cause that will be all that I will be thinking, as I watch over you all, even though I will be in Hell. Goodbye to all of my cousins, aunts and uncles, I was happy to have known you all even though some of you did not know me. Goodbye to my grandparents, I have always loved you. I wouldn't have ever changed you for the world. However, I was not like the rest of the grand-kids on either side, because I did not know how to show my love to you and I'm sorry for that, I could have tried harder. Goodbye to all the friends that I have

ever known, goodbye to this whole world and hello
to these pills that I am about to swallow...

**I WILL ALWAYS LOVE YOU ALL, AND I WILL
ALWAYS BE THERE FOR YOU WHEN YOU CALL.**

Why I Write

Rapoem:

I wrote **Rapoem** because I would always write lyrics to already made songs so I often wondered if I could write a whole song, so I tried it with this one. But as you will see it's not entirely done cause, there's no hook, but at least I tried.

<u>Rapoem</u>

Written For
Those Who Feel It

Verse 1:
I just wanna be successful
I'm tryna put myself on the map
Y'all see I write poems,
So, of course, I write raps
I'm tryna live it up big
In everything I do
Whether it be acting, rapping or writing
I'm tryna go there wit you
Let you see who I really am
And understand my perspective on things
Cause for me it ain't about the cars and cribs
Or the rock and the rings
It's about being an influence for the young
Provin' that if you keep God first, nothing can
go wrong
So take this journey with me through my life
thus far
Whether I make it or not, to me I'm still a star

Verse 2:
Fear is only as deep as you let it be
I fear for my mama's life
And how it affects my destiny
I love her to death
So if she wasn't around anymore
That wouldn't be much help

And I would put my life on the line for her to
have what I have
But if I don't have anything
She still gets half
Even though some of the things she does hurts
my heart
And since she has a bigger piece than most
She always hurts that part
And I try to talk to her about it
But some things she doesn't wanna hear
And because she ignores my advice
Where the rest of her life leads her is something
I will always fear

Verse 3:
I was born into a loving connection
That led to a hurtful one
Felt like a contagious infection
Of hurt and pain
That eventually moved to the separation
And quickly a divorce
Then a remarriage through adulteration
That is something I'm still trying to forgive and
forget
But it's hard when someone forces you into a
situation before its time
So I guess I learn to live wit regret
Because I never showed my true feelings
I knew they would never be together again
But the way it happened wasn't very appealing
So this is where I show my true soul
Because going through this gives me room to write
Kind of like my inspiration, or my light.

Why I Write

Somebody:

I wrote **Somebody** because there was a repetitive question around me. Why did I hold onto that guy so long even after he and a close person to me, had a thing after I told him how I felt about him. It was like right when I thought he was just a memory of my past, there was somebody there to remind me that he will never be forgotten. So I wrote it down to see who and why this kept being brought up and despite the ending of the poem, I had people in my life, bringing up the past like it was new news.

Somebody

Written For
Those Who Feel It

Somebody is getting on my nerves
Aggravating me up the hill, down the hill and
around the curve
Telling me things that I don't want to hear
Bringing up old shit that gets stuck between my
ears
Stuff about this dude that I finally got over
Keeping old feelings intact and putting the world
back on my shoulders
Talking about stuff that went on in the past
Things that make me wonder how long my "getting
over him" will actually last
It's like they want me to be stuck on this dude
for life
But he's moved on, got a baby on the way and damn
near a wife
Now I'm thinking about how things would've been
if we had got together
And forgetting that I realized that things turned
out for the better
At least on his part and hopefully mine too
Cause the whole time I was stuck on him, I was
using him as my excuse
To not get too close or fall too deep
Having him be the one to hold me back from taking
that leap
But I feel that I am ready to let him go and start
doing my own thing

But of course I have this little bee buzzing around with old news to bring
More mess about how he hollered at someone close knowing how I felt
Sometimes I wish that's not how the cards were dealt
But they were and yeah it burned
And now I take it as another lesson learned
Cause what can I say about that today
Oh my gosh, why am I still thinking of this dude in that way
Hopefully I will be strong enough to tell them to leave me the hell alone
Or ignore the crap about how he had my mind blown
Cause I'm tired of being reminded of stuff, knowing I should have been buried it
Its been past time to drop that load, considering how long I carried it
And maybe they will stop or let it die down
But most of the time, I hear this "somebody" when nobody is around
Now how in the hell could that possibly be
Damn.
I guess that "somebody" is me.

Why I Write

Virgin:

I wrote **Virgin** because I am a virgin at a lot of things, but the only thing most people hear when you're talking about stuff like that is I have never had sex. So I want you to read this and see what you take from it.

<u>Virgin</u>

Written For
The Inexperienced Ones

I am 21 years old and
I have never smoked weed
Because I know it's not what I need
To reach my goals, let alone succeed
And even if I follow my curiosity
I know it is something that my curiosity will
not plead
For cause, I'm a good girl and good girls do good
deeds
Try to remember that

I'm 21 years old and
I have never been in "real" love
Unless you count that love, I have for the man
above
Other than that, I have never had that hand in
glove
Fit and I've never felt the slug
Shots from another heart, or even had a reason
to buy an "I Love You" mug
Or even felt a passionate kiss or even a hug
Try to remember that

I'm 21 years old and
I have never legally driven a car
And when I did, it was never too far
Cause growing up I wasn't treated like a star
When it came to me, I was less than par

And that left a scar
And I take all my frustrations out at the bar
Try to remember that too

I'm 21 years old and
I have never had sex
I'm the one who is passed over for the next
That's why I become an ex
It's not that I don't want to take all of the steps
To get me there, trying to make the decisions to
or not to, keeps me quite stressed
But no matter what, I'm going to do what's best
For me

Now I know you will remember that.

Why I Write

I wrote **Answer's To ?'s** because I needed a voice of reason to help me figure out that I should just let those thoughts of that guy go. I saw myself not listening to actual advice, so I put together questions that I had, I answered them, read it back to myself and finally realized things turned out for the better on both sides, it just took me longer to see it.

This shit is very therapeutic.

Answer's To ?'s

Written For
Those Who Need It

Cause your friendship is too strong
As soon as you see right now you all aren't meant to be to be; it could stop now
Cause y'all grew up together, he's all you knew when you were going through the "liking boys stage"
Because he's all you ever knew
Maybe
He does
As friends, always and only God knows anything different
When you realize that he's not the only one out there for you
Yes
Yes, one day
If that's the way God has planned it
Yes, he didn't try to hurt your feelings before
No, you followed your heart and there isn't anything wrong with that
Because he feels embarrassed at the fact that he broke your heart
He's not sure if you will talk to him again
Living his life, as you should be
I don't think so
Unfortunately not
If it's written, when and if he discovers that you're who he really wants

Because your heart has shielded your eyes from
them
Because you don't want to hear it
No, it will always be there, just not as strong
Whoever God puts in that space
No, nothing is your fault, things happen sometimes
1:41 pm
Yes
Yes
Yes, that might be a good idea but I'll be here
for support either way
We just feel you, that's all
Maybe
I do.

<u>Why I Write</u>

I Got My Angel Now:

I wrote **<u>I Got My Angel Now</u>** because I was in a better place when it came to dating. I had finally gotten all the way over that other guy and I had finally stopped being so afraid of putting myself out there and I wanted to be bolder. I didn't even give my number out back then, cause I was afraid that the guy wouldn't like me but then he would still have my phone number and could crank call me if he wanted to or something like that. But this guy, seemed to be different, he was like my angel that swooped in to make all my hopes, dreams and wishes come true and for a while, he did.

I Got My Angel Now

Written For
Those Who Feel It

It's like he fell from the sky
An answer to a prayer I made a long time ago
He was everything I wanted in a guy
And it showed me how I was so afraid before
Because he came when I had doubt in my mind
It was like God had stopped listening
It was like love I would never find
Cause I shied away from everything that was
glistening
All the things that was good for me
Everything that seemed too far away
Not knowing what the outcome would be
Made my love life decay
Though I wasn't happy, I pretended I was
By making jokes and having fun
Watching everyone around me fall in love
I never thought I'd have a special someone
Hiding behind some things for so long
Like being inexperienced in a lot of areas
Made the idea of a relationship, wrong
So that's where I lived, behind the barriers
Until one day, I accepted a friend request
And gave out my number
Thought it was time for me to do what was best
So the rock that was on top of me, I climbed out
from under

Still didn't know if it would be right or
If I should take the chance
But I finally realized that this was something I
should fight for
If I wanted to find true romance
So I ignored the nerves in my heart that made me
stay lonely
And in return saw all the common interest we
shared
I pushed the bad feelings to the side and accepted
the good ones only
Cheesing at the fact that I had found someone who
genuinely cared he made me change for the better
You can't tell me I shouldn't hold tight
I was finally happy, knowing we were meant to be
together
Making me feel everything for once would be
alright
Out of all the devils I've met in the past
You may ask, how can I tell he's not one of them
How do I know he's the one that will last
Cause I have faith and I know a good one when I
see him
So though his wings are not visible to the
naked eye
I still feel like they are there
Ready to take our feelings to the sky
They are surrounding us everywhere
Covering this once scared little girl
Lifting our relationship off the ground
Through the clouds and around the world
Basically what I'm saying is I think I got my
Angel now.

<u>Why I Write</u>

Dreams:

I wrote **<u>Dreams</u>** because I just felt like writing something down. It's not really about anything specific, I just started describing something but made it sound like something else. See if you can figure out what those things are..?

Dreams

Written For
Those Who Feel It

You haven't had a pleasure
Closed tight like a box of treasure
That last longer than any time measured
Where it's wetter than the Sahara Desert

It's tighter than your hands can hold
Where you will find it surpasses any story told
And you will feel hot as hell in the winter's cold
It's like a poker game, even if you have the best
hand, it'll make you fold

It boggles the mind like a good magic trick
It will take more than three licks
To burn the fuel on this candle's wick
It exceeds the 1st round draft pick

Trust me; it's just what you need
So much pain that your heart will bleed
It'll have you on your knees ready to plead
It will get you higher than any strain of weed

Oh yes, it's way better than it seems
Thinking about it afterwards will still have you
hearing screams
A place where it always rains cream
And you'll be hooked just like fiends

One thing though, it only exists in our dreams.

Why I Write

Written Soul Part 2 (My Heart Beats):

I wrote **<u>Written Soul Part 2 (My Heart Beats)</u>** because I let this guy I used to know from the farmer's market, my brother and I used to work at, read the first **<u>Written Soul</u>** and he liked it. He wanted to see what happened with that, so I continued it, and this is what came out. He never got a chance to read the finished product, so maybe he's reading it now.

Written Soul

Part 2 (My Heart Beats)

Written For
You

My heart pulsates when I am near you
And I don't know how to make it stop doing that,
It's like it has a mind of it's own
Like it takes my brain,
While its controlling everything else,
Makes it quit working for them and uses it for
itself for the moment
I think my body would completely shut down if I
saw you everyday,
So I understand why that can't happen
And even though when you're around, she's around
I can't help how I feel,
How I've always felt
And no matter how hard I try to rid myself of
these feelings,
It only grows stronger with each sighting of you
And even though she holds my spot right now,
I believe that in another time or universe,
You are mine
And this is just Gods way of letting some of the
good
In these unimaginable times and places in our
minds
At this moment we live in now,
Seep through to let us know that there are
happier times out there
Somewhere

Now of course if there's a positive to that point
Then there has to be a negative
Which maybe I am living in now cause that is how
I feel
Or perhaps it gets worse
But I can,
No I will only live for what we have together
right here and now
Cause being friends is better
Than not having you at all
I still and probably always will
Love you.

Why I Write

Wishing On A Star:

I wrote **Wishing On A Star** because, well it was initially apart of Written Soul Part 2, but some people told me that it didn't sound right so I made it a separate poem. I wanted to reminisce about the past because back then, there were happier times. There were no thoughts of depression and trying fix it with negative things. I like to think how my life would've been if only we continued down the path that we thought was meant for us, not that I'm saying this life wasn't a blessing, leading to the point that we are at right now, but it's been a lot to handle. I wouldn't change anything, and I thank God for here and now cause we're still here and though we've been through these crazy, sometimes horrible things, we made it through and now its considered a lesson learned but there's nothing wrong with thinking about these things going a different way.

Wishing On A Star

Written For You

I sometimes wish things could be the way they were when we were younger before all the drama in your life began to cross the lines into my life and made me feel like I couldn't do anything to help you surpass your illness. As hard as I tried to help you then, being the shoulder you could lean on or having the hand to wipe your tears away, I feared that I was only making things worse. Then I left you alone in your darkest times cause at that time other people seemed more important to me; I made you go and turn to others that didn't have your back like I used to, and for that I apologize. I wish things could have been different but I see now that we both learned a lot from what transpired back then. You discovered trusting and depending on yourself, and I learned that I was too young to think that I could carry the burden of being your only support system. I'm happier with where we are now but those were some hard and depressing times for me and I'm sure for you too, cause that's when you fell into really bad habits over and over again. But you have overcome and I like to think that, even though I wasn't there physically, I was there mentally. With the words that I wrote down and sent to you, thinking to myself that I was hopefully encouraging you to leave all that crap in your past. Even if that's not true, just let me believe that because it hurt me to move away from you, for the reasons that I left and then soon after, hearing that you were falling further downhill. I cried a lot through those years. I wish they never happened the way they did back then because of the issues we both had with it, but without that we probably wouldn't be here, like we are today. Happy, blessed and living life free, the way it should be. But the times before all of that, when we were younger, when I didn't want to let you out of my sight in fear of never seeing you again, cause it seemed like time had stopped and everything in life would never be the same. So I would sit in front of the door hoping and waiting for you to show up. I missed you so much but when I did see you again, I felt like the clocks began to tick again and everything in life was the way it was supposed to be. There were no distractions of evil doings, going on around us cause there were none. The sky and walls weren't falling around us, no bowling alley rumors or postal romances, just happiness of being who we were and loving it. I miss those days. Why can't today be one of those days, only one of those beautiful days that anyone would like to have right now? No need for what ifs or wishing on stars cause its just one dream away.

Why I Write

Angel In Disguise:

I wrote **Angel In Disguise** because my Angel wasn't an angel at all. He seemed right at the beginning, but he eventually took his mask off, and his horns were showing. I think the whole time I knew him, he only told the truth once, and that was when he said he was a gang member, should have left then but the mask blinded me. If the truth was told, about anything else how was I to know cause he lied so damn much. So I thought to myself, if I can write a poem about how I thought he was the one, I can write one about why he was not.

So here goes.

Angel In Disguise

Written For
The Next Girl

I know y'all saw me going on and on about the
"Angel" I found
Basically bragging about having someone with the
mutual feelings at last
Saying how he was the best guy for the job, I had
seen around
And how he made me leave all the crap, I was
afraid of in the past
Just being all around happy
Sitting back letting destiny do what it do
Finally seeing and doing what I thought was best
for me
But I should have known it was too good to be true
Cause here I am trying to unmask him
I've always said that there's a reason why you
call someone your ex
Usually they haven't changed, so what's the point
of going back with them
He just makes me so mad when he says he's going
to call or text
And doesn't
So then out of anger I start to write something
like this
Telling him I'm being patient even though I knew
I wasn't

Thinking about all the time I was wasting and opportunities I might miss

Cause he won't communicate, it feels like he's leading me on

I mean I knew it was going to take time but damn, this is hard

I've been through something like this before and I ended up in love alone

So I don't plan on backtracking when we've come so far

I just can't get over the fact of him saying one thing and doing another

How in the hell do you smell the scent of a rose that won't grow

Meaning how am I supposed to be with someone who makes me feel like it'll never go further

I mean he said he changed his life to be with me, which I'm happy to know

But because I'm so inexperienced with dating

I don't know if he's being sincere or

If he was afraid to tell me that his feeling for me were slowly fading

Maybe it's fate making sure I don't fall too fast or too deep like I did before

Helping me see that he's just practice for the real thing that I hope is coming soon to a "Monica" near you

Even though I wanted him to be the one

Either way I'm ready, I feel my time is long overdue

Like I don't think I can keep doing this, it's not fun

But I guess this has to happen each time so the bad gets weeded out

They say "the 3rd times, the charm," and that's two down

The first was the other guy I write about
But you know I can say whatever, when I know
sometimes I think about that one but he's still
just a friend now
It's just, this one seemed like he was the one to
make me stop searching and in a way he was
Cause I see, what going out looking for it, kept
making me find
So now I'm waiting to be found by love
Cause I'm tired of wasting my time
You know thinking back, I see now that he was the
wrong guy when we started
But I was blinded by his appearance and all the
things we had in common, which made me ignore
the lies he told
Cause I was so happy that I might have finally
found what everyone around me has, unlocking the
chains on my heart that was once heavily guarded
I didn't want something so small to come in the
way of such a big moment, not thinking of the
drama that was down the "ignorance" road
Even with this happening he says he wants to get
out of the "friend zone"
But the way he's going about it, shows otherwise
Maybe if I wasn't being so dumb I would have been
gone
It's a Doobie (a wrap) for me but until he uncovers
himself he'll just continue to be that Angel in
disguise.

Good luck to the next girl.

Why I Write

Powerless To Powerful:

I wrote **<u>Powerless To Powerful</u>** because this is something that I found in one of my notebooks from when I first started writing and I saw how powerless I was when it came to the guy I'm always writing about, how I gave him the power to control my heart from falling for someone else. It was a complete waste of time, but without it, I wouldn't have seen how powerful I could be. But despite my feelings back when I wrote this, I have nothing but love for that guy, I still consider him a friend, and I hope he does well in all that he does in this life.

Powerless
To
Powerful

Written For
He Who Held The Power

I push all guys away cause of an experience that I went through. This guy hurt me; HE HURT ME!!! The way he just moved me to the side like my feelings didn't matter, it just made me fall apart. I wanted him, and I wanted him to want me, but because we were friends first, he didn't want me to feel the pain that might have come with that and end up jeopardizing that place that we were in as friends. However, little did he know, the way he told me that it would never happen and his actions after, with someone that was close to me, hurt me way worst. I mean it brought about a pain that would affect my whole life. If height measured self-esteem from the ground to the sky, mine was the Earth's core, and he made it that way by choosing her. So now when I meet men, some pleasant well most of them lovely but I can't ever think to see them as anything but a friend let alone get serious with anyone of them cause HE is who I want PERIOD. Why can't he see me as I think he should? Damn, I hate this man but you will never see me act out or tell him that cause I have developed a great defense mechanism. I know that one day it will come out and he will know how he changed the way I deal with men because of that day, and we will have the conversation that we should have had a long time ago, maybe on that particular day where he decided she was better than me. I wish it never happened, I don't regret having met and been friends with him, but I wish I would have shared my first love with someone that wanted to share it back with me, hey it's a good thing that we didn't have sex. But I guess that experience was something I needed to go through and grow from and so far I'm still learning how to.

Now with that said, today in 2011, I'm okay with him turning me down back then cause he wasn't ready for someone like me and I was nowhere near prepared for how he was back then. I'm happy I went through that cause it helped me with my writing, all the things I have written about him helped me get through it all. Now finding a guy that will share my feeling and will be the one for me, well I'm taking baby steps with that. I thought I found him a few times and you know how that goes but I'll find him. It'll happen for me, when it's right, I know that now.

Here in 2015, I'm still Powerless. Still trying to deal with the situation of basically feeling like I could be passed over for the next girl, by all men. I mean, granted most men are dogs but I mean, someone I like, and it feels like we could honestly have something real. That guy, (^HIM^) made me think that there was someone else that was better than me and now I'm here, afraid that, that's the general mindset of any man that's interested in me. So I beat you to the punch,

by pushing you away. See, an excellent defense mechanism. But I know that if it's meant to be, the right guy will break down my walls and help me get over all of the self-esteem issues I didn't know I still had, but apparently, I do.

<u>My Thank You's</u>

First and foremost, I love how this creative way of getting feelings out, has trickled down through both sides of my family and hit me square in the heart. I hope this project inspires the next generation in my family and empowers someone to continue this gift.

I want to thank the being that made me so creative, my <u>Lord and Savior</u>. Poetry is one of the gifts that He has bestowed upon me. Without Him, I wouldn't be here or able to express myself in such a fantastic way.

My family, is my whole heart, and this is why I say that:

<u>My mama</u>, <u>LP</u>. I honestly couldn't imagine life without you, and I don't want to. No one will ever be as close to me as you are, you are the best-est best friend, anyone can ever have. You believe in everything that I strive for, and I sincerely couldn't ask for anything more than that. That's why when I write about you, there is so much love in each word because you have a massive part of my heart and you always will.

<u>My daddy</u>, <u>LJ</u>. Even though we don't often get along because we are almost the same person, you have helped me through a lot. You let me live with you and pay not one cent of rent, for years, despite my attitude and laziness. Yeah, we got on each others nerves but we also had a lot of great laughs, and good times and I honestly wouldn't change any part of our relationship. When I thought I

didn't need or want your approval or opinion, as I grew older, I realized that wasn't the case. You have taught me a lot about this world and who I want to be in it.

  My brother and sister, L&C. What can I say
      about these two? Everything, (laughs).
  I'm telling all the secrets, (laughs), just kidding. All
  of our secrets will remain secrets, from my end.
  Okay, so let us start with <u>my sister</u>. You remind
  me a lot of daddy and I feel like that is why we
  don't get along. It's like our relationship goes more
  in-depth than sibling rivalries. But when its good,
  its great. The only thing is that "great" doesn't
  last long. Maybe I envy how independent you are,
  and perhaps you envy how much I could care less
  about what people think about me? Either way,
  we are slightly divided and I don't want to be.
  Now <u>my brother</u>. You were my second official best
  friend, behind mama, of course. I looked up to you
when we were growing up, then things changed. It's like
our personalities switched, you used to be so outgoing,
and I was this shy little girl that tried to follow you
wherever you went until I could no longer chase after
you and your friends. Don't get me wrong, I'm still shy
in certain situations, but I am more willing to be out,
in the world. You, however, you're more introverted.
We get along when we haven't seen each other for a
  while, but that doesn't last long either, (laughs).
    I love you both and will do anything within
        my power, for the both of you, and I
        know y'all will do the same for me.

<u>My step-family, C, F and my niece, T.</u> I hate calling
y'all that, but I feel I have to separate the two, so

people will understand my life better. I love everybody the same cause we are family, and I'm glad we are. C, I was probably the toughest one to reach cause I was so into my mama, still am, but you stuck with it and got it done. I love the way you stepped in to be a mother figure but not to take anyone's place, you helped out a lot, and I appreciate you for that. F, we agreed on a lot of things back in the day. Not to say that we don't still agree on things now but in those days, I needed someone on my side and you were there, especially when things seemed like they were going downhill within a specific union but it worked itself out. Also, without you, there would be no···

T, my one, and only niece. My Adidas buddy, even though you still wear that other brand, from time to time but if you stick with me, I'll get you entirely on The #3StripeTeam one day. I'm proud of the young lady you are becoming, even though you are still learning to be the person you want to be and it has taken you through some things, you've been very mature about letting the right people know about it. That's something special. Kids these days are nothing like that, hell, most of my generation wasn't like that. You're going to be somebody special in this world if you believe you can be. You will always have a supporter, right here.

My Grandparents, W&J. Oh, how I miss my grandpa, and I wish I were closer to him before he passed, I am glad that we got to tell each other that we loved each other before he became one of the best guardian angels. I am delighted that I have the chance to have a better and closer relationship with my granny, though. You are the original tomboy (laughs). Because of you, most of the females in our family are more comfortable in sweatpants and a t-shirt instead of a dress or a skirt· _L&M·_ I have lived next door to your house, almost my whole life and for some reason, when I was younger, going to visit, just wasn't the move to make· I am glad that my mind changed, once I grew up, and I hate that it took so long for me to realize how fun y'all were· No, not because I was getting paid to do things for you guys but because that was the truth· I miss granny so much, I know she would be proud of me, for finally getting a job and following my dreams when it comes to this poetry thing· Hey, granny I bought a house, I wish you were here to see it in person· Grandpa, you are a mess, I think because of you I can tell a joke with a straight face, (laughs)· I know lately, we haven't seen much of each other, but when we do, I already know what to expect: "I'm still trying to find a job from 11a-12p with an hour break," (laughs)· Last but not least, _Barbara·_ I didn't know you that well but I do remember that you were funny, and you were very stuck in your ways· We didn't share many conversations and now that you're gone, I wish that we did· Even though you five were and are from top to bottom, different people, and we've had and continue to have a special separate bond with each other, you all mean and have meant the world to me, equally·

My aunts and uncles, all together but genuinely separate· All of you have taught me to live life to the fullest, be the best me I can be and always to remember that family is and will continuously be forever· There are a few in there that I really don't know what kind of person I would have turned out to be, without you and I know, you guys know who you are. Love everybody.

The cousins, the best people to have by my side growing up. The saying is "We're not friends, we're cousins" but y'all are the only real "friends" I ever had and needed. Some of us have had moments that weren't the best but those moments inspired me to realize this gift, and because I wrote my experiences down, I got over a lot. Hopefully. All of you can do the same if you haven't already and not take anything to heart cause everything happens for a reason and I believe that these things that happened to me was to see what and who were really important to me, God, myself and my family.

My close friends and extended family, I wish I could shine a light on everyone individually but I have taken up too many pages already. I appreciate and love you all, if it weren't for you, I would not be me. You all have forced me to experience life very differently, and because of that, you have all inspired all of this, and I can share my gift with the world, so I can hopefully inspire someone else with my story.

I also, want to thank those family members that helped me with my poetry, even though you admittedly didn't want to (laughs). Oh and to my #3Stripe4Life clan, I thank you for your help too. Definitely for the markings seen in standard lighting as well as under the "black light". I appreciate and love you all, tremendously.

Thanks for purchasing and reading.
Now go and inspire the world to be better

Extra's

A Crazy Day

~*Echo* – 21-year-old, female college student
~*Boo* – 11 years old, female. Sister to Terry, one of the kids in the house
~*Terry* – 12 years old, male. Brother to Boo, the other kid in the house
~*Louder* – 20 year old, female. Neighbor and friend to Echo
~*Uncle Marques* – The kid's uncle.

Situation:
As we follow Echo, a 21-year-old student at Central Piedmont College, as she gets off the bus and is walking home from the bus stop only to find that someone broke into her house and from the sound of it, they're still there. Playing.

(Echo walks into the door and sees two
kids running around in her house)

Echo:

(To herself) What the heck?

(Walks back outside to make sure the address
is right, then walks back inside)

Echo:

Man, what the heck are y'all little niggas doing in my house?

(Boo and Terry stop playing and look at Echo
as if she just walked into their house)

Terry:

Um, sorry but we didn't think anybody lived here.

Echo:

> Wasn't the door locked, I mean how the heck did y'all get in here?

Boo:

> Yeah, the door was locked but we had a key. See, we used to live here. I'm Boo, and this is Terry.

Terry:

> Yeah, and when we came in, the house was just like we left it, so we started playing with our toys.

Echo:

> The locks are not the same, besides I have lived here my whole life and I've never seen y'all before.

Terry:

> I think that you're mistaking, the address is 6010 right?

Echo:

> Yeah!

Boo:

> Farn Pon?

Echo:

> Yeah!! (Thinking to herself and mouths the words what the hell?)

Terry:

> Well then, this is the house. Maybe something happened to you when you were younger, and it gave you amnesia, and you couldn't remember moving.

Echo:

> What did you say little nigga? Nothing like that ever happened to me. I think I would've remembered.

194

(Boo says to Terry)

Boo:

Maybe she doesn't know what (puts up quotation marks with his fingers) "amnesia" means.

(Echo bends down to Boo and Terry)

Echo:

Do you know what (puts up quotation marks with her fingers) "suck something" means?

(Terry and Boo both nod in agreement)

Terry and Boo:
Yes.

Echo:

Then whenever you're ready, I'm ready and y'all are already on your knees so whenever is good for me.

Boo:

Man look, we're sorry that we just broke in but we didn't think anyone stayed here.

Terry:

Yeah, we'll call our parents.

Echo:

Yeah, where are your parents, how did y'all get here?

Terry:

Our parents stay in Florida. It will take a while for them to get here.

Echo:

WHAT!!! (puts her hand on her forehead and walks around in a circle)

Boo:

> Yeah, we ran away from home. We took a cab from the airport, here.

Echo:

> Okay, you ran away from home... You know y'all are in Charlotte?

> (The kids look at each other as if they don't
> know what Echo is talking about)

Echo:

> You know that Charlotte is the name of a woman, but it's also a city in North Carolina?

Boo:

> Yeah, yeah, we know, didn't we say that we used to live here?

> (Boo whispers to Terry)

Boo:

> Man Terry, she is slow.

> (Terry nods in agreement)

Echo:

> I heard that, and from the looks of this situation, it seems that y'all are the slow ones.

Terry:

> Look, man can we use the phone or not?

Boo:

> Man, we ain't gotta ask her nothing. We lived here first.

> (Front door opens)

Echo:

> Yeah (Boo walks off to the kitchen, to use the phone) and you Boo Boo or whatever your name is, you can shut it before I kick your...

(Terry follows behind Boo as she begins to dial the number)

Echo:

> Little ass

Louder:

> "As if" (laughing), I love that movie. Hey Echo, you got that movie? I know you do cause I saw it here.

Echo:

> Man, what the heck? Why is everybody just walking into my house like we are on the street and I'm a bum in a box?

Louder:

> Man, what are you talking about, who else is here?

(Talking in the background)

Louder:

> Oh, you in here trying to get your freaky freak on, eh? Okay, well I just came for the movie.

Echo:

> What movie? Man, I don't have any movies.

Louder:

> I know you got Clueless here, I saw it in the den (starts walking towards the hallway).

(Boo and Terry are still talking on the phone in the background)

Echo:

> Man, I don't know, look for it...

Louder:

> (Cuts her off) Hold up, what the heck was that?

Echo:

> (Looks around like she doesn't know what Louder is talking about) I don't hear anything

> > (While Echo is talking, you hear Boo and
> > Terry talking in the background)

Louder:

> Listen, you idiot. There it is again

> (Echo listens and hears Boo and Terry talking on the phone)

Echo:

> Oh, that's the kids

Louder:

> KIDS!!! I didn't even know you had kids, you didn't have them yesterday. What you do, adopt?

Echo:

> No nigga, what the heck?

> > (Boo and Terry hang up the phone and come
> > back to where Echo and Louder are)

Louder:

> Oh, hey little ones. Is your mother treating you right?

Terry:

> Yes.

Louder:

>See, the kids never lie (chuckles).

Echo:

>Whatever, did y'all get in touch with your parents?

Boo:

>Yeah, they said they were going to send our uncle to get us.

Echo:

>Okay, how long will that take?

Boo:

>Not long, he lives right down the street.

Louder:

>Oh. What's his name cause I've lived down the street all my life, maybe we stay near each other?

Boo:

>Okay and who are you?

Louder:

>Oh, excuse Echo, she's not a very good host. Louder is the name (sticks her hand out for handshakes).

Boo:

>What in the world kind of names do you all have?

Terry:

>Yeah, who named y'all?

Louder:

>Look little brats. My real name is Lasagna

Terry:

>LASAGNA!?!?

Louder:

>Yeah, my mama loves Italian food, and she had been craving it while she was in labor with me.

>(Boo and Terry laughs)

Louder:

>But when I met Echo, I changed it cause I was tired of kids picking on my name.

Terry:

>Louder is what you chose? Why, exactly?

Louder:

>Well, I figured that you would have to talk louder to have an echo, so that was it.

Boo:

>You are just a little slower than Echo.

Echo:

>Yo, whatever. What's your uncles name?

Terry:

>His name is Marques.

Louder:

>Okay, I know everybody on this street, and there's no Marques' that comes to mind.

Boo:

>It has to be. His address is 7314.

Echo:

>Hey Louder, ain't that your address?

Louder:

Heck yeah and like I said before, I've lived here all my life.

Terry:

Okay, there's got to be a mistake, because that can't be.

Boo:

Maybe she has amnesia too.

Louder:

What!? I don't have amnesia.

Echo:

Yeah and neither do I, punks.

Louder:

Are y'all sure the street name is right?

Terry:

Yeah, we asked Echo.

Echo:

Yeah, it's Farm Pond.

Boo:

FARM POND!?!?!?

Terry:

We said, Farn Pon

Louder:

See, stupid people talking to stupid people makes a stupid conversation.

Echo:

Alright (waves hands to hurry the kids), well go call your parents back, so they can call and catch your uncle. We don't want the people, whose house he shows up at, to call the cops on him cause he's looking for little kids. Tell him to come here.

(Boo and Terry rush to the phone)

Louder:

Man, if I hadn't come here, you would be stuck with those kids for life because you're too stupid to think that the street name wasn't right (laughing).

Echo:

Whatever man. But what I want to know is how the cab driver got them here if they said, Farn Pon?

Louder:

Man them niggas are kids, they can't get a cab by themselves.

Echo:

Well, that's what they said.

(Boo and Terry enters back into the room)

Terry:

We called. Our parents caught our uncle in time. He's on his way over here.

Boo:

Yeah, they said it's going to take 20 minutes.

Louder:

Well, now that that's over I guess I will get the movie and be out.

Echo:

Hope you have fun finding it because I've never seen it here

Louder:

> Whatever man its here, I saw it

> (20 minutes pass. Knock on the door)

Echo:

> Who is it?

Uncle Marques:

> I'm here for the kids, I'm their uncle.

Echo:

> Okay (opens the door and the kids walk up).

Terry:

> Sorry about the misunderstanding.

Boo:

> Yeah but we appreciate your hospitality.

Echo:

> No problem, y'all be safe (stands in the doorway).

> (Rumbling in the background)

Louder:

> Yes, I found it!

Echo:

> See y'all (waves goodbye as they walk to the car and closes the door as Louder walks back into the room). What the heck? It took you 20 minutes to find... (looks at the tape), man this ain't even Clueless.

Louder:

> Yeah, I know. I couldn't find it, so I got this instead (pulls up the tape to her face).

Echo:

> (Laughing) Man that's

Louder:

> "Kill The Man"

Echo:

> I've never even heard of that before.

Louder:

> Yeah, I know. I got it from home.

Echo:

> What?!? You know what, I don't even wanna know. I've had a stressed day already.

Louder:

> Yeah, I know what you mean, I'm Audi 5000.

Echo:

> Alright, see ya. Close the door and lock it behind you, I don't want any more unexpected guests.

Louder:

> Alright mane (starts to close the door but quickly opens it back up). Aye, was the kid's uncle light skin?

Echo:

> (Looks back, shakes her head and sighs).

Louder:

> What? (closes the door and you hear her mumbling on the other side of it).

(Scene goes black)

The End

Printed in the United States
By Bookmasters